Teachers' Beliefs about Corrective Feedback and Their Classroom Practice

小学英语课堂教师纠错性反馈信念与实践

张晓华 著

东北师范大学出版社
长 春

图书在版编目（CIP）数据

小学英语课堂教师纠错性反馈信念与实践 / 张晓华著. —长春：东北师范大学出版社，2020.12
ISBN 978-7-5681-7331-5

Ⅰ. ①小… Ⅱ. ①张… Ⅲ. ①英语课—课堂教学—教学研究—小学 Ⅳ. ①G623.312

中国版本图书馆CIP数据核字（2020）第247264号

□责任编辑：徐小红　刘玥婷　□封面设计：言之凿
□责任校对：刘彦妮　张小娅　□责任印制：许　冰

东北师范大学出版社出版发行
长春净月经济开发区金宝街 118 号（邮政编码：130117）
电话：0431-84568115
网址：http：//www.nenup.com
北京言之凿文化发展有限公司设计部制版
北京政采印刷服务有限公司印装
北京市中关村科技园区通州园金桥科技产业基地环科中路 17 号（邮编：101102）
2022年6月第1版　2022年6月第1次印刷
幅面尺寸：170mm × 240mm　印张：9.25　字数：216千

定价：45.00元

我所全方位认识的张晓华

（代序一）

接到晓华老师的书序邀请时，我还在美国佐治亚州立大学访学。听闻她的硕士论文即将出版发行，我由衷地为她高兴。晓华老师这么多年的勤奋终将收获丰硕成果，对她来说，这样的荣誉可谓实至名归！

晓华是我五年前指导的硕士研究生。初识晓华是在教育硕士的课程班上，第一次上课我就对这个灵性十足、好学且热情的学生印象深刻。更令我惊喜的是，这名聪慧的学生具有超强的理论联系实际的能力。对所学的复杂的教育理论知识，她都能灵活地联系课堂进行解读。枯燥的理论在她的解读下变成了有趣的教育实践。有着超强学习能力和清晰逻辑思维的晓华在研读硕士期间各科专业成绩突出。她所撰写的硕士毕业论文得到领域内专家的高度评价，并被答辩委员会全票评选为“年度优秀论文”。

《小学英语课堂教师纠错性反馈信念与实践》这一选题是现行教育研究的热点之一，具有积极的现实意义。更难能可贵的是，这是一项实证性研究。作者深入一线课堂，通过细致的课堂观察和反复的访谈，收集并整理出丰富的数据。在对这些数据解读的基础上，作者对纠错性反馈课堂中的教师实践和教师理念进行了科学的分析和总结。这本书的问世是教师反馈研究领域的一项重要成果，它对广大教育工作者，特别是一线英语教师有着积极的参考作用。本文结构规范，论证逻辑清晰，对英语专业的学生及研究人员来说，也是一本优秀的写作范文。

这么多年来，晓华一直是我的骄傲。她的勤勉使得她在研究和教学的道路上步履稳健。此外，生活中的晓华还是远近闻名的贤妻、良母和孝媳。借以此序祝福晓华享受研究，快乐生活！

陈 锫

2018年3月

陈锫（女）

深圳大学副教授，毕业于澳门大学和上海外国语大学。研究方向为：英语应用语言学、英语教育学、英语课堂教学教法等。编写专著《实践中的任务型教学：现状与展望》（2011年），并持续在国内外核心期刊发表科研论文。其论文曾荣获中国社会语言学优秀论文奖（2008年），中国基础英语教育论文一等奖（2009年），外研社杯全国基础教育论文二等奖（2010年、2011年）等奖项。此外，她还承担各级各类科研项目，自2008年起独立承担并主持教育部社科项目（项目名：任务型教学在中国）。指导语言学及教育硕士研究生，并承担研究生课程的讲授，如主讲教育硕士课程——学术论文阅读与论文写作。

爱钻研的人儿最美丽

（代序二）

2015年11月，齐放教授和我指导的深圳大学首批英语教育硕士钟颖的专著正式出版，我俩为之作序。现在，陈锫教授和我指导的英语教育硕士张晓华的专著《小学英语课堂教师纠错性反馈信念与实践》即将出版，我感到特别高兴，并欣然为之写序。

《小学英语课堂教师纠错性反馈信念与实践》一书，把研究的视角盯在小学英语课堂上教师纠错这个环节，对小学英语教师纠错性反馈的理论和方法进行了探讨与分析，提出了一些个人见解，很有价值，对其他小学英语教师的课堂纠错行为有很强的指导意义。

在学习过程中，学生犯错是很正常的，更何况小学生呢？因此，在小学英语课堂上，如何对待小学生在学习英语时出现的错误是值得每个小学英语教师思考的。张晓华老师在专著里讨论的“纠错性反馈”，说到底就是一个小学英语课堂教学中的评价问题。课程改革至今，小学英语教学评价一直是我们面对的难题。张晓华老师提出的“纠错性反馈”，体现了《义务教育英语课程标准（2011年版）》对英语教学评价提出的基本理念：小学的评价应以激励学生学习为主，评价方法的合理性和多样性等。

我始终认为，作为英语教育硕士，研究问题固然重要，但更重要的是要学会如何做研究。包括如何选择课题，如何查阅文献资料，如何做调查，如何写分析报告等。作为小学英语教师，在繁忙的教学之余读硕士，其最重要的提升，我认为就是研究能力的提升。张晓华老师的专著就是她研究能力提升的表现。

最后，我想说的是，读完硕士不是学习的终点，而是新的起点。希望张晓华老师把在学习过程中学到的新知识、获得的研究能力运用到自己的教学工作中去，并取得新的成绩。

是为序。

禹　明

2018年3月

禹明（男）

中学英语特级教师，深圳市政府特殊津贴专家，全国优秀外语教师园丁奖获得者。系教育部全国教师教育课程资源专家委员会（第二届）委员，教育部“国培计划”首批英语培训专家，教育部《义务教育英语课程标准（2011年版）》综合审议专家，深圳大学英语教育硕士生导师。

实证研究“纠错性反馈”助力英语教学

（自序）

近几年，纠错性反馈因其对英语口语发展起到极其深远的促进作用，逐渐在国内外成为二语习得备受关注与流行的一个研究热点。但是，目前还缺乏相关的实证研究，少见有英语作为外语背景下的教师纠错性反馈的信念与他们的课堂实践的相关研究，更难找到研究者走进一线教师课堂做相关实证研究，而这对提高英语教学非常有意义。本研究将通过课堂观察与教师访谈来探索教师纠错性反馈的信念与他们的课堂实践之间的关系。

这是一项在深圳市一所小学开展的个案研究。研究者为了选出有代表性的教师个案，经过三个缜密的筛选阶段，最终确定四名教师代表作为被研究者。从2014年4月至同年7月，研究者对每一位被研究教师开展四次访谈，并听他们每人三节英语课。最后，一共录制了12节课并撰写了16个访谈，并进行编码、分析，分别收集到四位教师的19、15、12、14个纠错性反馈教学案例。研究者主要用定性分析所得数据资料。主要的研究结果如下：

第一，英语教师拥有如下几方面的纠错性反馈信念：他们认为纠错性反馈是对学生英语学习非常有帮助的重要教学策略。在英语学习中，学生出现错误是很正常的。然而，教师喜欢对所有书面错误进行纠正，而认为对口语错误没必要所有都纠正。他们共同的理由是：当学生在努力尝试用英语表达自己的观点时，应将交流与理解放在第一位，而且教师纠错时还要注意不伤害学生的自尊心。教师着重鼓励学生主动参与课堂和重复纠正同一错误类型以加深学生记忆。纠错聚焦在知识难点与学生屡次出现的错误上。

第二，英语教师纠错性反馈实践概括如下：教师非常热衷于设计与组织纠错性反馈教学活动。Jane收集所有学生的错题并回顾往届学生的出错情况，结合起来认真仔细地为纠错性反馈教学做好准备。Vincent和Claire尤其注重鼓励学生参与纠错活动，所以他们的学生在同伴互相纠错方面表现比较突出。老师们对纠错性反馈的种类喜好不尽相同，最常见的纠错种类是重铸策略。纠错聚焦频率最高的是语法语言点。当学生在用英语进行口语交流时，教师能如他们在访谈中提到的，将理解与交流放在第一位，能克制自己，不去给学生纠错。

第三，四位教师的纠错教学信念在很大程度上能与他们的教学实践相统一。Thompson于1992年发表言论：实践与信念的关系就如一条双行道，不单单信念影响实践，实践也反作用于信念。本研究结果显示出这样一个趋势：教师的教学理论知识越扎实，他们越能更好地开展纠错性反馈教学实践，学生越能有效地学习。

基于以上研究结果，研究者进一步概述通过研究得到的启示与研究存在的不足，然后对未来的研究提出建议。

张晓华

2019年3月

PREFACE

In recent years, corrective feedback (CF) , due to its potential role in facilitating oral English development, has become a hot and popular research topic in Second Language Acquisition both abroad and domestically. There is, however, still a lack of related empirical studies. There is little investigation into language teachers' beliefs about corrective feedback in English as a foreign language (EFL) contexts, and it is hard to find researchers who come closely to the first-line teachers' classrooms to do the empirical research which is very meaningful for improving EFL teaching. This research explores the relationship between EFL teachers' beliefs on CF and their instructional practices by observing and recording the classes and interviews.

This is a case study conducted at a primary school of Shenzhen City. Four teachers were finally selected as the case teacher participants (Ida, Vincent, Claire and Jane) after three phases of the selection process with the researcher's deep consideration. The researcher gave each participant four interviews and observed three of their English classes from April to July, 2014. Finally, twelve lessons were video recorded and a total of sixteen interviews (three observations and four interviews for each teacher) were transcribed, coded and analyzed. There were respectively 19, 15, 12 and 14 pieces of CF examples arising. The qualitative analysis was mainly adopted for the research. The major findings are summarized as follows:

EFL teachers hold these kinds of beliefs about CF: They treat CF as a very helpful and important teaching strategy for students' EFL learning. Errors are naturally existing during EFL learning. Nevertheless, they prefer to give CF to students' written errors and some of the spoken errors instead of all the spoken errors.

Their common reasons are that comprehension comes first when students are trying their best to express their ideas in English, and teachers should try not to undermine students' self-esteem when giving CF. They placed their emphasis on students' active participation and repeating the same error correcting strategy. The foci of CF should be focused on the difficult knowledge points and students' frequently existing errors.

EFL teachers practice CF in this way：They designed and organized CF teaching activities with great enthusiasm. Jane collected all students' errors and recalled the errors her former students had, and prepared her lesson's CF activities carefully with great passion. Vincent and Claire, in particular, provided opportunities and encouragement for their students that were engaged in CF situations, and the students behaved more actively in correcting peer students' errors. They had different preferences of CF types, and the most common type of CF used was recast. The most common linguistic target of CF was grammar. All four teacher participants refrained from giving CF when students were engaging in their oral communication, just like they stated in the interviews that comprehension came first at that moment.

The four case teachers' beliefs about CF were largely congruent with their CF teaching practices. Thompson argued in 1992 that the relationship between practices and beliefs is a two-way street. Not only do beliefs influence practices, but also beliefs can be shaped by practices. A trend emerged from the results of this study here：the more theoretical knowledge about teaching the teachers had, the better they implemented CF practices and the students learned more effectively.

Based on the results, the researcher also summarized the implications and limitations of this study, and put forward some suggestions for future studies.

CONTENTS

CHAPTER 1 INTRODUCTION

CHAPTER 2 LITERATURE REVIEW

CHAPTER 3 METHODOLOGY

CHAPTER 4 RESULTS AND DISCUSSION

CHAPTER 5 CONCLUSION AND IMPLICATIONS

APPENDIXES

CHAPTER 1

INTRODUCTION

Research Background

1. The Original Intention of the Research

In recent years, corrective feedback (CF) , due to its potential role in facilitating oral English development, has become a popular research topic in second language acquisition abroad (Chu, 2011) . CF has also become popular both in oral and written English development among researchers and teachers in China. Studies of second language (L2) classroom interaction have attracted much attention in SLA studies since in SLA studies since the 1980s. Corrective feedback in L2 classrooms lies at the core of research on teacher-student and student-student interaction (Lyster & Ranta, 1997) .

Second language acquisition (SLA) researchers have different opinions on CF. Some hold the opinion that CF is necessary (White, 1991) because it can match the learners' utterances with their corresponding versions in the target language and draw the learners' attention to structures that have not been mastered, thus, initiating a learning process. Some researchers advocate abandoning CF in classroom interaction due to its limitations. A number of studies have examined whether CF is effective (Doughty & Varela, 1998; Long, Inagaki & Ortega, 1998; White, 1991; Bohannon

& Stanowics, 1988; Demetras, Post & Snow, 1986; Farrar, 1992; Saxton, 1997）. There has been a growing interest in the role of CF in SLA in the last decade（Ellis, Loewen, & Erlam, 2006）. A number of descriptive studies based on data collected in classrooms（Panova & Lyster, 2002; Sheen, 2004）and on data collected in a laboratory-type setting（Iwashita, 2003; Mackey, Oliver & Leeman, 2003; Philp, 2003）have examined the types of CF received by learners and the extent to which this feedback is noticed by the learners.

Interest in teachers' beliefs has also spread into the field of SLA（Borg, 2003; Richards, 1998）. The foci of early research on teachers' beliefs have largely been on the general pedagogical beliefs（Johnson, 1992）, covering the areas of reading and literacy. The common conclusion is that teachers' beliefs influence teachers' in-class behaviors（Johnson, 1994）. Narrowing down the scope of research on teachers' beliefs and practices to a specific area will make it possible to see if there is a match between their beliefs and classroom practices; however, there has been little investigation into language teachers' beliefs about corrective feedback in English as a foreign language（EFL）contexts, and it is hard to find researchers come closely to the first-line teachers' classroom and do the empirical research, which is very meaningful for improving language teaching, especially EFL teaching.

Taking both of these two interesting issues into account, this thesis investigates the relationship between EFL teachers' beliefs on CF and their instructional practices by observing and recording the classes and interviews.

2. Teaching Oral English at the Primary School Level

According to the English Curriculum Standard, it is clear that the basic requirement for primary English postulates the main aims are to develop students' interest, self-confidence, and positive attitudes towards English learning, to cultivate the pupils' language sense and enable good pronunciation and intonation, as well as to develop the pupils' preliminary ability to use English in daily exchanges laying a good basis for further English study（2011）. As seen above, English teaching in

China's primary schools has entered a new era, which focuses mostly on the usage of the language, or in other words, the importance of spoken English.

At present, there is a "dumb English" phenomenon existing in the practice of English teaching of primary school in China. Generally speaking, most students' ability to express themselves is not high. Moreover, they are not able to use English to express their own ideas exactly. Teaching English with the exam-orientation concept is not advocated, especially in primary schools. The common concept accepted by most people nowadays is to pay great attention to oral English teaching at the primary school level.

3. Why Oral CF to Students Is Needed

Most English learners often face language fossilization in their English studies, which prevents their progress from taking place, which is labeled as "fossilization phenomenon" by researchers (e.g. Selinker 1972). To avoid this fossilization phenomenon, the most effective and important method is to give oral CF to English learners when their errors exist. Oral CF is indispensible in students' English learning, especially at the very beginning of the learning step called primary school English learning level.

Purpose of This Study and Research Questions

Firstly, the purpose of this study is to investigate teachers' beliefs about corrective feedback by the use of the qualitative method. Secondly, it is to elicit teachers' interpretations of the use of CF in primary schools. Lastly, it is to assess the possible gap between teachers' beliefs and their practices, which aims to gain some ideas about stimulating the development of EFL teaching in Shenzhen.

The study addresses the following three research questions according to the purpose stated above.

(1) What beliefs do EFL teachers hold about corrective feedback?

(2) How do EFL teachers practice CF in actual primary English classrooms?

(3) To what extent are EFL teachers' beliefs about corrective feedback congruent with their observed teaching practices?

The first question aims to provide a picture of what beliefs the EFL teachers hold about CF by several interviews. Through answering this question, the researcher tries to expose the EFL teachers' current pedagogical views. Also, it is imperative to study teachers, as a very important guide in language studies, whose perceptions are essential to the research. Their CF beliefs are the major research area. The second research question deals with EFL teachers' real-life implementation of CF in primary school English language learning classrooms. Their performing of CF in their practical English classrooms is another major research area. The last research question focuses on the relationship between the EFL teachers' beliefs and their practices about CF. Through answering this question, the researcher explores the intricate relationship between perceptions and performances of CF in interaction involving primary school EFL teachers.

Significance and Motivation of This Study

The study will take up Borg's call（2003）for investigations that address specific aspects of language teaching in relation to teacher cognition. The specific aspect of teaching that will be considered is CF. The aspect of cognition to be examined is teachers' beliefs.

There is a lack of empirical research on language teachers' beliefs about corrective feedback in EFL contexts. Therefore, the study aims to contribute to the enrichment of the knowledge about EFL teachers' beliefs about corrective feedback and their practices in primary school classrooms while enhancing our understanding of ELT pedagogy and the curricular situation.

The study of teachers' beliefs has in the last 15 years emerged as a major area of enquiry in the field of language teaching. This study will focus on the relationship between teachers' beliefs and their classroom practices. More specifically, there has been interest in the extent to which teachers' stated beliefs correspond with what they do in the classroom, and there is evidence that the two do not always coincide（e.g. Karavas-Doukas, 1996）. Such differences have been viewed as an undesirable or negative phenomenon（and described using terms such as incongruence, mismatch, inconsistency, and discrepancy）. In this study, the author argues for a more positive perspective on such differences, which the author conceptualizes as "tensions", i.e. "divergences among different forces or elements in the teacher's understanding of the school context, the subject matter, or the student"（Freeman, 1993）. More specifically, the author examines divergences between what English language teachers say and do in corrective feedback, and, by exploring the reasons for these, also provides insight into deeper tensions among competing beliefs that teachers hold. The perspective on the study of tensions we advance here positions them as a valuable focus for both research and teacher development.

Corrective feedback is an important issue for teachers' teaching and learners' learning in every subject. Teachers often have many ideas about their teaching and students' learning, but most of the time their practices are not congruent with their beliefs. Thus, the author wants to focus on this topic, which is related to teachers' stated beliefs about CF and their practices. Most importantly, the study hopes to assist the front-line teachers in a successful understanding of their own teaching beliefs and practices about CF. The finding of this research indicates that teachers and their beliefs towards CF are the key factor facilitating or retarding the implementation of CF. Based on the significant finding, the researcher provides some recommendations for EFL teachers in China.

Overview of the Thesis

This thesis consists of five chapters. The first chapter, as is shown above, introduces the background of the research, explains teaching oral English in primary level and why oral CF to students is needed, clarifies the purpose of the study and the research questions, summarizes the significance of this research, and lastly presents an overview of the thesis.

Following this introductory chapter（Chapter 1）, Chapter 2 reviews the literature on the major research areas in this study. It begins with a historical overview on teachers' beliefs and their practices abroad and in China both theoretically and empirically. The second part focuses on a definition of feedback and CF, the types of CF, and research on CF abroad and in China. The next part is an overview on the definition of teachers' beliefs and sources of teachers' beliefs. And then come another two parts, which are teachers' beliefs and their classroom practices on CF. At last, the researcher turns to the linguistic targets of errors.

Chapter 3 explains the research methodology and data collection procedures. This chapter starts with a detailed description of the research context and the participants' selection. The third part focuses on the research instruments, which is followed by two sections. They are semi-structured interviews and classroom observations. Then the detail of data collection procedures is given. At the end of the chapter, this study procedure is provided and summarized with detailed explanations.

Chapter 4 presents case study results focusing on four participants. Based on the framework of a set of research questions, each case study is interpreted. Four case studies are used to ascertain the relationship between participants' beliefs of CF and their actual performance in English classrooms. To begin the case study section, the schooling contexts are introduced. Each case study includes three parts. The first part is the participants' background information. The second part is the participants' performance and perceptions of CF. The following part deals with the cross-case analysis. The end of the chapter then provides the common and different information of the four case studies.

The final chapter of this thesis summarizes the findings of the research. The three research questions that are the core elements of this study are first addressed. Then the researcher gives some possible suggestions to improve teachers' English teaching. Finally, she summarizes limitations of this research.

CHAPTER 2

LITERATURE REVIEW

Historical Overview

Lots of research has been done on teachers' beliefs about teachers' practices abroad and in China both theoretically and empirically. Most research on teachers' beliefs focuses on how teachers' beliefs influence their instructional practices. Researchers have assumed that teachers' beliefs influence the way they design their classes.

(1) Richards and Lockhart (1994) stated that it was important to study the relationship between teachers' beliefs and classroom practices. They claimed, "What teachers do is a reflection of what they know and believe." Richards (1998) also stated, "A primary source of teachers' classroom practices is the belief system: the information, attitudes, values, expectations, theories, and assumptions about teaching and learning that teachers build up over time and bring with them to the classroom."

(2) Many researchers try to examine the extent to which teachers' beliefs affect their teaching practices. For example, Johnson (1992) investigated the relationship between ESL teachers' beliefs and their actual classroom practices. Smith (1996) examined the relationship between decision making and beliefs of ESL teachers.

(3) Zheng and Davison (2008) investigated what happened to teachers when the country promoted a new curriculum in secondary schools. The result of the study tells us that English teachers in China are bound by textbooks, and serve as transmitters of grammatical knowledge.

In general, studies about teachers' beliefs have already become a rather significant part of EFL research. Moreover, research on CF in language instruction has developed tremendously over the past two decades. A considerable amount of varied research in the field has contributed to the theoretical understanding of second language acquisition. Much in-depth research on the effectiveness of CF in benefiting second language learners has been done, which also proves the value of CF in language teaching. DeKeyser（1993）pointed out that error correction was really a controversial issue in second language acquisition, because it was often subsumed under the general term "negative evidence". In fact, corrective feedback, error correction, negative evidence, prompts, negative feedback, and focus on forms are all different labels, which refer to the same language teaching issue called "how competent speakers react to learners' language errors"（Lyster, 1997）.

Based on the previous studies, the present thesis intends to explore the relationship between teachers' beliefs about corrective feedback and teachers' practices.

Corrective Feedback

1. Definitions of Feedback

Oxford Intermediate Learner's English-Chinese Dictionary defines feedback as "information or comments about something that you have done, which tells you how good or bad it is". In English writing teaching, it refers to any comments or information given to the writers either by their teacher or by other learners in terms of a writing task. In oral English teaching, it refers to any comments or information given to the speaker either by their teacher or by other learners in terms of an oral task.

2. Definitions of Corrective Feedback

The effectiveness of corrective feedback is mainly attributable to the negative evidence it entails. Language learners have access to two types of input (Gass, 1997) : positive evidence and negative evidence. Positive evidence informs the learner of what is acceptable in the target language (Li, 2010) and contains "the set of well-formed sentences to which learners are exposed" (Gass, P36) . Negative evidence, in contrast, provides the learner with information about the incorrectness of an L2 form or utterance and is often realized through the provision of corrective feedback in response to the learner's non-target like L2 production (Li, 2010) .

Ellis (2009) stated that corrective feedback constituted one type of negative feedback which took the form of a response to a learner's utterance containing a linguistic error.

Truscott（1996）defined negative feedback as “correction of grammatical errors for the purpose of improving a student’s ability to write accurately”.

3. Types of Corrective Feedback

Lyster and Ranta（1997）identified six corrective strategies, which were recasts, explicit correction, clarification requests, metalinguistic feedback, elicitation, and repetition, whereas Panova and Lyster（2002）added one more — translation. The six types of corrective feedback, which were first reported by Lyster and Ranta（1997）, have been widely accepted by other studies. The definitions of the six CF strategies are listed below together（Lyster and Ranta 1997：46—49）.

（1）Recasts involve the teacher’s reformation of all or part of a student’s utterance minus the error and are generally implicit.

（2）Explicit correction refers to the explicit provision of the correct form. As the teacher provides the correct form, he or she clearly indicates that what the student had said was incorrect.

（3）Clarification requests indicate to the students either that their utterance has been misunderstood or that their utterance is ill-formed in some way and that a repetition or reformulation is required.

（4）Metalinguistic feedback contains either comments, information, or questions related to how well-formed the student’s utterance is, without explicitly providing the correct form.

（5）Elicitation refers to techniques that teachers use to directly elicit the correct form from the student.

（6）Repetition refers to the teacher’s repetition, in isolation, of the student’s erroneous utterance.

Examples of the six types of corrective feedback are showed in Table 1 below（Chu，2011）.

Table 1 Examples of the six types of corrective feedback

Types of CF	Examples of the Six CF
Explicit correction	St: She take the bus to go to school. T: Oh, you should say she takes. She takes the bus to go to school.
Recast	St: She take the bus to go to school. T: She takes the bus to go to school.
Elicitation	St: She take the bus to go to school. T: She ...? T: How do we form the third person singular form in English? T: Can you correct that?
Metalinguistic feedback	St: She take the bus to go to school. T: Do we say she take? T: How do we say when it forms the third person singular form?
Clarification request	St: She take the bus to go to school. T: Pardon me?
Repetition	St: She take the bus to go to school. T: She take?

4. Research about Corrective Feedback Home and Abroad

Doughty (1994) found that teachers finely tuned CF to adult second language learners in the same way that parents do in their interactions with their children and that the learners noticed the teachers' feedback. These findings led SLA researchers to focus on the relationship between learners' errors, the CF provided to them and their responses to the CF. Lyster and Ranta (1997) and Lyster (1998) investigated CF in an immersion programme at a primary school. Recasts occurred most frequently, although the uptake rate after recasts was the lowest at 31%, while uptake after the other forms of CF was 50% or more (Lyster & Ranta, 1997). The grammatical and phonological errors of learners triggered teachers' recasts more often compared to other errors（Lyster, 1998）. Most of the teachers' recasts were similar to non-corrective repetitions and this made the recasts ambiguous to the learners（Lyster, 1998）.

Mackey et al.（2000）found that recasts occurred most frequently after morpho-syntactic errors in Japanese as foreign language（JFL）classes at a university, who examined the interactions between adult English and Italian learners as SL, FL and native speakers. Lyster（2004）found that the provision of CF, such as clarification requests or elicitations in communicatively oriented SL classrooms of an immersion programme, was more effective for the learners' improvement in written tasks compared to recasts. Panova and Lyster（2002）compared adult ESL learners' perceptions of CF between learners of higher and lower proficiency. Recasts happened most often, and proficient learners noticed recasts better than less proficient learners. These previous studies vary in a number of ways, such as the learner population（children or adults）, the interactional contexts where CF occurs and the teaching styles in the programme（form-oriented or meaning-oriented）. These factors seemed to trigger the varied results of the studies, such as the CF types that were found to occur frequently or the effectiveness of CF. According to Oliver（1995）, the interactional context influences types of CF and the rate of learners' modified output following the CF in children's ESL classrooms. The CF occurred most frequently in exchanges where the focus was on language, while recasts occurred most often in exchanges where it was on content. The rate of modified output after CF was the highest in the language-focused exchanges.

Although CF is gaining more and more prominence abroad, it has not drawn enough attention inside China. Teachers' CF and learners' uptake are the few issues addressed in studies in China in the EFL classroom in primary and middle schools（Zhao, 2005）and CF strategies are used in oral English classrooms（Zhu, 1996）. Zhao's study（2005）examined CF and uptake behavior at three different proficiency levels, which were classrooms in primary schools, junior and senior schools, and which concluded that negotiation of form was more preferred than recasts in correcting lexical and phonological errors, moreover, in response to grammatical errors, EFL teachers provided different CF strategies according to different proficiency levels of the learners. Hu's study（1995, 2005）elicited the opinions and attitudes of both teachers and students by questionnaires and interviews: firstly, how often errors were treated; secondly, what types of errors were treated; lastly, how errors were treated.

Teachers' Beliefs

1. Definitions of Teachers' Beliefs

There is lots of research about language teaching and learning. There are also a large number of words that have been used to describe beliefs such as perceptions, opinions, attitudes, theories, and ideologies（Woods, 1996）. Different definitions from different scholars' perspectives can be found.

Doctor Chen（2010）of Shenzhen University clarified, "Teachers' beliefs play a major role in defining teaching tasks and organizing the knowledge and information relevant to those tasks."

Zheng and Jiang（2005）defined teachers' beliefs as "representing a mixture of personally constructed explicit and implicit opinions of language and language learning, serve as a mediator for experiencing, negotiating and responding to the environment".

Borg（2003）described teachers' beliefs as practical system of mental constructions that were held by teachers. They are dynamic, defined and redefined on the basis of educational and professional experiences throughout teachers' teaching lives.

Richardson（1996）stated that teachers' beliefs were "an individual's understandings of the world and the way it works or should work, may be consciously or unconsciously held, and guide one's action".

Following the previous definitions, the author redefines teachers' beliefs as a system of guiding theories that are teaching methods and strategies, teachers' role, students' role, classroom management, teaching renovation and self-improvement. These theories have a great impact on teachers' practices in the classroom.

2. Sources of Teachers' Beliefs

Teachers' beliefs are shaped and influenced by several factors including their experiences of teaching and learning, pedagogical knowledge, professional education, and working context (Carter, 1990).

Richardson (1996) identified the following three categories of experience which influenced the development of beliefs and knowledge about teaching. They are personal experience, experience of schooling and instruction, and experience with formal knowledge.

Generally speaking, there are three major sources of beliefs. The first source is teachers' schooling. Teachers' learning experience helps them shape their beliefs about teaching most of the time. Their success and failure in the process of learning can help them improve their beliefs to some extent. The second source is teachers' personal experiences, which can contribute to the development of their personalities. Teachers' beliefs are greatly influenced by teachers' personalities (Tsui, 2003). The third source is professional training. This knowledge includes teachers' knowledge of the subject, teachers' understanding of theories, their knowledge of classroom management, and their abilities and skills in classroom interactions with students (Tsui, 2003).

Teachers' Beliefs and Their Classroom Practices

Although opinions are divided on the exact definition of teachers' beliefs, it is generally acknowledged that teachers' beliefs exert great influence on their classroom practices. Teachers' beliefs lie at the very heart of teaching. Pajares（1992）stated "Few would argue that the beliefs teachers hold influence their perceptions and judgments, which, in turn, affect their behavior in the classroom".

Previous studies have used several instruments to compare the extent to which teachers' stated beliefs are correlated with their practices. Some studies have proved the consistency between teachers' beliefs and their practices. Johnson（1992）studied the fit between the "theoretical orientations"（in terms of methodological preferences）towards teaching ESL literacy of three teachers and their instructional practices over a number of lessons. The result indicated that ESL teachers holding clearly defined theoretical beliefs provided instruction consistent with their theoretical orientations. Smith（2002）found in a Canadian study of ESL teachers in post-secondary classes that teachers' instructional decisions were highly consistent with expressed beliefs. The teachers with a structured grammar-based view of language selected different goals from the teachers with a functionally based view of language. From Gu's（2009）case study on Chinese primary and middle school English teachers, it is obvious that the repertoire of knowledge of beliefs guide teachers in their own learning and professional development as well as in their handling of the multifaceted nature of classroom teaching.

Added to this and in contrast, a large number of studies have found inconsistencies between teachers' beliefs and their practices. Yim (1993) found in studying ESL teachers in Singapore, that while they were able to articulate beliefs about the role of grammar teaching from a communicative orientation, these beliefs were not evident in their classroom practices that were driven more by structured grammar activities of a non-communicative kind. A study by Rayana Saad and Saouma BouJaoude (2012) likewise showed that no consistent relationships between teachers' beliefs, views of the nature of science, and classroom practices were found.

Corrective Feedback and Teachers' Beliefs

Not much literature can be found addressing these topics. Schultz (1996) conducted a survey to investigate foreign language (FL) students' and teachers' views on error correction and the role of grammar. Results indicate that students' favor focuses on form. 90% of the students surveyed agree that when they make errors in speaking they would like their teachers to correct them, whereas only 2% of the students agree that teachers should not correct them. Conversely, only 30% of the teachers surveyed agree that when students make errors in speaking the target language, they should be corrected; 41% of the teachers disagree. After reporting the findings, Schultz (1996) presented "it might be wise to explore the fit of learners' and teachers' beliefs and take into account their opinions of what enhances the learning process". This statement supports the significance of investigating teachers' beliefs in the process of students' learning. This notion was echoed by Basturkmen (2012) when he stressed the importance "for an understanding of teachers' thinking in relation to on-line decision making in the classroom".

Linguistic Targets of Errors

Language errors can be classified from different perspectives according to different standards. Researchers categorized language errors in different ways. Chun et al. (1982) and Chenoweth et al. (1983) carried out studies that helped to shed some light on the issue of how different types of errors were treated. In their study, they divided errors made by non-native speakers into five types: discourse errors (errors beyond sentences level) , factual errors (errors concerning factual knowledge or truth value of utterances) , word choice errors (errors involving incorrect choice or addition of a noun, verb, adjective, adverb, preposition, question word or other types of functional words) , syntactic errors (errors of tense agreement, morphology and word order) and omissions (errors involving the incorrect omission of nouns, verbs, auxiliaries, articles or other words required by rules of standard English grammar) .

The study takes into account three of the five error types put forward by Lyster (1998) . Lyster (1998) investigated the relationship between error types and feedback types in four French immersion classrooms. The nine hundred and twenty-one learners' errors were coded as grammatical, lexical, phonological, or as unsolicited uses of the first language (English) . However, Lyster examined the last type, unsolicited uses of L1, only because they were interested in them in the French immersion classrooms. In fact, they were not errors. Also in Chinese EFL classrooms, uses of L1 (Chinese) are inevitable. Therefore, unsolicited uses of L1 are not included in the error types in the current study.

CHAPTER 3

METHODOLOGY

Research Context

This study was conducted in Shenzhen, which is a young city at the forefront of economic reform in China. As an open and modern city, Shenzhen plays a leading role in reforming and adopting new thoughts, including primary education reformation. Many primary schools in Shenzhen use similar teaching materials as their counterparts use in Hong Kong, especially the English textbooks. More importantly, they keep in touch with Hong Kong's advanced teaching theories and methods. The research will be carried out at Yucai No.3 Primary School, a school attached to Yucai Education Group. It is a public school with professional teachers, and it is famous for its English teaching and activities called Weekly English Show. It is located in Shekou, Nanshan District. There are several reasons for choosing this school. Firstly, it is a highly recommended school in Shenzhen with a good reputation. Secondly, the school follows the national curriculum, but innovatively teaches its own curriculum. Most importantly, the author of this paper works in this school and manages the English teaching department. So, it is convenient for the author to do the research.

Primary English for China by Longman Press is the general English textbook for most of the primary schools except some international schools and foreign language schools in Shenzhen, but many schools have selected their own supplementary English teaching materials to meet students' diverse demands and to improve their language proficiency level. All the English teachers in Yucai No.3 Primary School have supplementary teaching materials for their students, for example, English newspapers, reading books, storybooks and so on. Whereas, it is learned that *Primary English for China* plays a predominant role in the teaching process and other materials serve in subordination.

Participants

For the purpose of making the study more objective and choosing the participants most likely to represent the whole group of teachers, the researcher chose the participants carefully using three phases in the process. The first phase was to ask all the English teachers in Yucai No.3 Primary School whether they were willing to participate in this research or not, to gain some participant candidates. The second phase was to check the participant candidates' language teaching theoretical beliefs by using Johnson's (1992) research achievement, which distinguished the language teachers' theoretical beliefs into three approaches: skill-based approach, rule-based approach, and function-based approach. John (1992) concluded that almost all of the language teachers had clear beliefs, and all of these three approaches could well represent almost all of them. The third phase was to reduce the number of participants to only four. Why did the researcher choose four participants instead of two or three or another number of people? The researcher had her own consideration. Firstly, she wanted to choose the participants to represent different EFL teachers who had different theoretical beliefs. Secondly, she needed the participants to represent different ages' EFL teachers. Thirdly, the teacher participants must be hard-working and have a great deal of accomplishment in EFL teaching at school. The detail of the three phases would be shown below.

Phase 1: Asking teachers' willingness to be participant candidates.

There are a total of 11 English teachers in Yucai No.3 Primary School. The author explained the study and also invited the teachers to join in the study in one teaching and research meeting. All of the teachers were willing to take part in the author's research. So, ten EFL teachers finally took part in the research during the first phase "characterizing EFL teachers' theoretical beliefs". All of the ten subjects were teaching English from Grade One to Grade Six. Nine teachers are Chinese, and one is from America and students call her foreign English teacher. These teachers had taught EFL for an average of eleven years. All of them held teaching certificates in the area of EFL elementary school education. All ten teachers held bachelor's degrees, whereas one held a master's degree. The following Table 2 shows a summary of the teachers' personal information.

Table 2　The Ten Teacher Participants' Background Information in Phase 1

Name	Age	Degree	Years of Working	Sex	Teaching Grade	Number of Teaching Class	Number of Lessons / Week	Nationality
Jihan	23	Bachelor	1	F	Grade 2 to 6	11	11	American
Sarah	24	Bachelor	1	F	Grade 3	1	12	
Ida	27	Master	3	F	Grade 2	3	14	
Vincent	33	Bachelor	11	M	Grade 5	2	12	
Helen	34	Bachelor	12	F	Grade 1	3	14	
Helena	35	Bachelor	13	F	Grade 3 and 6	3	14	Chinese
Claire	36	Bachelor	14	F	Grade 2 and 5	3	14	
Sisi	38	Bachelor	15	F	Grade 4 and 6	3	14	
Tracy	39	Bachelor	20	F	Grade 1 and 2	3	14	
Jane	43	Bachelor	21	F	Grade 3 and 4	3	14	

Phase 2：Checking ten candidate teacher participants' theoretical beliefs.

A Multidimensional EFL Theoretical Orientation Profile was designed to gather information about teachers' theoretical beliefs across two main separate measures and one ancillary descriptive material of what each teacher believes to constitute an ideal EFL instructional environment that was used to do the further analysis (Johnson 1992) . The two main separate measures included:

(a) A belief inventory of theoretical and pedagogical statements which reflect each teacher's theoretical beliefs about EFL learning and teaching.

(b) The selection of what each teacher believes to be an appropriate instructional lesson plan. The two measures and the description were administered during a 15 to 40-minute private meeting between the researcher and the teachers.

Beliefs Inventory (Leu&Kinzer, 1991) was the first task. It contains 15 statements, five of which represent each of the methodological approaches toward second-language teaching (see Appendix 1: The form received by the teachers was corrected slightly. The three teachers' theoretical beliefs terms were canceled.) . Here the researcher used it as the EFL teachers' beliefs inventory tool. Johnson used it in her research in 1992 and she invited two expert raters to validate the 15 statements and the two expert raters had done some rewording and recoding to make them more effective.

The researcher asked the ten teachers to read all of the 15 statements and select the five which most closely reflected their own beliefs about EFL learning and teaching. And the teachers got a percentage score based on the number of skill-based, rule-based, and function-based statements they selected. The three approaches would be explained below.

Johnson (1992) investigated the relationship between ESL (English as a second language) teachers' beliefs and their actual classroom practices. She found that most of the language teachers had clear beliefs: skill-based approach, rule-based approach, and function-based approach.

(1) Skill-based approach emphasizes the mimicry, memorization and repetition of native language patterns, utilizes drill and practice to generate language production, and separates language study into four discrete language skills: listening, speaking, reading, and writing (Johnson, 1992). This approach originates from the empiricist explanation (Bloomfiled, 1942; Lado, 1964; Rivers, 1964). It assumes that language learning is a mechanical process of habit formation resulting from behavioral and conditioned responses with the target language.

(2) Rule-based approach views second language learning as a process of rule-governed creativity, allows comprehension of the language to precede language production, and treats all aspects of language learning as part of an interrelated whole (Johnson, 1992). This approach originates from the rationalist explanation (Ausubel, 1968; Carroll, 1966). It asserts that language learning is an innate ability which combines the intellectual understanding of language as an intricate system of grammatical structures with the desire to communicate within meaningful contexts.

(3) Function-based approach focuses on the use of authentic language within situational contexts, provides functional language use, and emphasizes meaningful communication over correct structural form (Johnson, 1992). This approach originates from the communicative explanation (Halliday, 1973; Hymes, 1972; Littlewood, 1981; Widdowson, 1978). It places language learning in a social context of interaction in which the learner must become a participant in real-life contexts.

Lesson Plan Analysis (Stempleski & Rice & Falsetti, 1986; Kinzer, 1988; Johnson, 1992) was the second task. It presented teachers with three separate instructional lesson plans, each one was designed to teach the same grammatical concept, which are the modals can, will, may and might. But each lesson plan reflected one of the three methodological approaches (see Appendix 2: The form received by the teachers was recoded slightly. The three teachers' theoretical beliefs terms were canceled.). All of three lesson plans were validated by two of Johnson's invited expert raters. All of the three lesson plans received 100% agreement by the two raters and were incorporated into this task without modification.

The researcher asked the ten teachers to read all of the three lesson plans carefully and select the one which best reflected their own beliefs about EFL teaching. After completion of this task, the teachers were assigned either a skill-based, a rule-based, or a function-based code according to the type of lesson plans they selected.

An analysis of the results of the Multidimensional TEFL Theoretical Orientation Profile identified three distinctly different profiles (Johnson, 1992). And they were operationally defined as dominant, dual and multiple theoretical orientation (see Table 3). A dominant theoretical orientation was designed as two sides. One side is to select at least four out of five (80%) consistent statements on the Beliefs Inventory. The other side is to have a consistent selection on the Lesson Plan Analysis task. A dual theoretical orientation was operationally defined as those teachers who: (a) selected statements on the Beliefs Inventory (two or three out of five) that reflected both of those methodological approaches, or (b) selected a lesson plan that was inconsistent with the Belief Inventory and they formed two main orientations. A multiple theoretical orientation was operationally defined as teachers who: (a) selected statements on the Beliefs Inventory which reflected two approaches, and (b) selected a lesson plan which was inconsistent with the two approaches based on the Beliefs Inventory.

The results of the beliefs inventory of the ten teachers would be shown as the following. None of the ten teachers was found to have dominant theoretical orientation. Eight of the ten teachers (80%) were found to possess theoretical orientation that reflected the presence of two methodological approaches. Five teachers (50%) held theoretical orientation which combined the skill-based and function-based approaches. Two teachers (20%) reported a combination of the rule-based and function-based approaches in their theoretical orientation. One teacher (10%) was identified as possessing both the skill-based and rule-based approaches in her theoretical orientation. Two of the ten teachers (20%) were found to have multiple theoretical orientation.

The following Table 3 shows the results of the Multidimensional TEFL Theoretical Orientation Profile based on the two separate measures.

Table 3 The Results of the Multidimensional TEFL Theoretical Orientation Profile

Theoretical Orientation	Subjects		Beliefs Inventory Scores (%)			Lesson Plan Selection	Results
	Years of Teaching EFL		Skill-based	Rule-based	Function-based		
Dominant							None
Dual	Sarah	1	40	20	40	Skill-based	Skill / Function-based
	Helen	12	60	0	40	Skill-based	Skill / Function-based
	Helena	13	40	40	20	Skill-based	Skill / Rule-based
	Jihan	1	20	40	40	Function-based	Rule / Function-based
	Ida	3	60	20	20	Function-based	Skill / Function-based
	Vincent	11	60	20	20	Function-based	Skill / Function-based
	Claire	14	20	40	40	Function-based	Rule / Function-based
	Tracy	20	40	20	40	Function-based	Skill / Function-based
Multiple	Sisi	15	20	40	40	Skill-based	Skill / Rule / Function-based
	Jane	21	40	40	10	Function-based	

Phase 3: Confirming the four participants chosen.

The results of the Multidimensional TEFL Theoretical Orientation Profile analysis indicated that the majority of these EFL teachers (80%) had dual theoretical orientation, 20% of them had multiple theoretical orientation, and none of them had dominant theoretical orientation. This result is quite different from the result of Johnson's research in New York which indicated that the majority of those ESL teachers (60%) possessed clearly dominant theoretical orientation. And most notably, Johnson's findings showed that the frequency of dominant theoretical orientation clearly favored the function-based approach. And this research also found that although none of the teachers had dominant theoretical orientation, most of them (90%) clearly favored the function-based approach. This finding is consistent with the changes and innovations in EFL teaching which have occurred in recent years in Shenzhen, or even among China as a whole. More and more teachers notice the importance of using English for communication in daily situations. Therefore, the function-based theoretical orientation may represent EFL teachers' overwhelming popularity approach at the present time in Shenzhen. Although China's traditional education concepts and examinations still have great impact on teachers' teaching practices and they cannot clearly have one dominant approach, they have a clearly changing tendency now.

Four teachers from the ten participants were chosen and continued to finish the later research. The selected teachers to participate in this study were Ida, Vincent, Claire and Jane. The four subjects' selection was based on the result of the statement survey of beliefs inventory and the lesson plan selection of "characterizing EFL teachers' theoretical beliefs". Of the five teachers (50%) identified as having the skill-based and function-based approaches, the researcher chose Ida and Vincent. Of the two teachers (20%) identified as having a combination of the rule-based and function-based approaches, Claire was chosen. And of the two teachers (20%) identified as having multiple theoretical orientation, Jane was chosen. And these four participants were of different ages, ranging from their twenties to forties. They all possessed an enthusiastic work ethic and produced great teaching results. Most importantly, they were all popular among the students.

Table 4 The Four Teacher Participants' Background Information in Phase 3

Name	Age	Degree	Years of Working	Sex	Teaching Grade	Number of Teaching Class	Number of Lessons / Week
Ida	27	Master	3	F	Grade 2	3	14
Vincent	33	Bachelor	11	M	Grade 5	2	12
Claire	36	Bachelor	14	F	Grade 2 and 5	3	14
Jane	43	Bachelor	21	F	Grade 3 and 4	3	14

Instruments

The researcher explored the interface between teachers' actual corrective feedback performance and their beliefs of CF through an analysis of classroom interaction and interview comments in four case studies. A combination of observations and interviews provided the most appropriate source of data. This combination of data provided both perceptions and performance surrounding the issue of CF at the micro-level of primary school English classroom interaction. Erickson (1996) called this type of approach "micro-ethnography" or "ethnographic microanalysis", and argued that in order to understand the subtle aspects of interaction which were often socially organized (Hymes 1972, 1974) , it was necessary to directly analyze interaction in detail.

Case study is a study of a bounded system, emphasizing the unity and wholeness of that system, but confining the attention to those aspects that are relevant to the research problem at the time (Stake, 1998) . Case study methods allow researchers to consider the influence of complex interactions between contexts and people within and across the setting of teacher education (Miller, 1994) . They also allow researchers to investigate how and why similar phenomena occur across contexts (Miller, 1994; Young & Halleck, 1998) . Case study methods also support a consideration of interactions among individuals and program goals in multiple contexts (Young & Halleck, 1998) .

Observation of classrooms by the researcher has long been considered a laudable way to collect research data (Market, 2000, p. 179) . In this study, classroom observation had been used to gain relevant information of the four case participants' CF practices. And interviews were used to get information of the participants' CF beliefs.

1. Semi-structured Interviews

The semi-structured interviews were carried out with the four participants from April to July in 2014. Four semi-structured interviews were carried out among the four teacher participants. The first and second interviews were before each teacher participant's three classroom observations. And the third and fourth interviews were after the observations. Each interview began with the youngest participant Ida, who is the most cooperative and active, and also very intelligent. The researcher made improvements on the interview questions after interviewing Ida each time for the purpose of making the interviews more efficient and all-sided.

The aim of the first semi-structured interview was to elicit the teachers' beliefs about teaching English（see Appendix 4）. And then, the researcher gave the four participants another semi-structured interview in order to investigate the teachers' attitudes towards giving correction to students' errors. The content of the interview was based on Kavaliauskiene and Anusiene's survey statements about students' attitudes towards correction of errors（Kavaliauskiene & Anusiene, 2012）. And the author made some changes in order to investigate teachers' attitudes towards CF. It contained nine questions that required the four teacher participants to think and answer（see Appendix 5）. Before the third semi-structured interview, the researcher gave the participants an explanation aiming to introduce the six categories of corrective feedback（see Table 1 to know the training content）, and it was the precondition of the third interview. The aim of the third interview was to elicit the participants' stated beliefs about corrective feedback in their daily teaching（see Appendix 6）. After the data collection, the fourth interview would fulfill all the data and analysis（see Appendix 7）. In order that participants felt comfortable talking with the interviewer, each interview was conducted both in Chinese and English for about twenty minutes in the teacher's office. A recording pen was needed to record the interview data. And shorthand notes were taken during the interviews. The accurate interview questions were designed beforehand. They were modified after the interview with the youngest participant Ida each time. Apart from the designed questions, questions according to the actual situation were timely asked in the interviews.

2. Classroom Observations

Merriam (2009) stated that at least three reasons could account for researchers' preference to take classroom observation as a research instrument. There have been hundreds of studies using classroom observation since 1970s. Firstly, classroom observation allows researchers to collect more precise and detailed first-hand data in a naturalistic classroom setting. Secondly, classroom observation can record some special moments, which may provide basis for the follow-up interviews. Thirdly, classroom observation is the best choice when participants are not willing or able to share their opinions about the ongoing study. On account of the three reasons, the researcher applied classroom observation as one of the main research instruments.

After the first and second interviews, the researcher discussed with the four teacher participants to decide when and how to observe each one's three lessons. It's important to know each teacher participant's general course schedule and teaching plans. The researcher also learned about each teacher participant's respective extra teaching materials besides the common textbook which played a very important role in language teaching before the first formal classroom observation, so that the researcher would integrate into each participant's class soon. The researcher gained some suggestions from Bogdan and Biklen (1992) for the early days of classroom observation. First, have the participant introduce you. Second, keep the students undisturbed and comfortable as usual. Thirdly, don't explain explicitly and exactly the purpose of the study. As for the last suggestion, the researcher aimed to explore the teachers' natural use of CF, so that the researcher did not inform the participants the details of the study. The researcher just informed the participants that she wanted to observe three of their lessons for the purpose of getting some information of their teaching, because the researcher was the leader in charge of the school's English teaching.

The researcher observed each participant's two open classes and one common class between May and June in 2014. The open class was usually well prepared and much more successful. The common class was often authentic and natural. The open classes were video-recorded, but not the common classes. The classroom observation was "semi-structured" in the sense that the researcher focused on the proceedings of the class events as a whole instead of specific activities in the classroom. This enabled the research to "capture more meaningful class events than determining in advance what to look for in the observed context"（Seliger & Shohamy, 1989）. In other words, the research paid attention to three dimensions at the procedural level — interaction between the teacher and the individual student or students, pair work and group work. Interaction between the teacher and the individual student or students means the exchange of information between the teacher and the individual student or students, or we can say that it's the questioning and answering pattern. Pair work here means the talk between two partners. And group work here usually means talking in a group of four or six students.

When observing the class, the researcher sat at the back of the classroom and took notes on the events of the class. Each lesson lasted for forty minutes. The researcher did not involve herself in any classroom activity so that the observation would not disturb the teachers' normal teaching process. The researcher found out when, what and how with regard to corrective feedback in the classes（see Appendix 3）, and immediately following the observations, the researcher reviewed and expanded all notes to include further information and details. These notes assisted the researcher in data transcription and data analysis to a great extent. The data was transcribed as soon as each class ended in order to ensure the data's accuracy and validity.

Procedures of the Study and Data Analysis

This part's aim is to explain the research design and the process of the data analysis. For the sake of validity, the researcher invited Fiona, a second-grade graduate student of Shenzhen University, to be the second researcher. Fiona's major is also English Teaching and she also has great interest in CF. She is a hard-working and smart girl. The researcher's supervisor recommended Fiona as a great helper. Fiona knew none of the teachers and nothing about their daily teaching, which meant that she had no pre-positioned information in her mind. So Fiona and the researcher first observed the classes and analyzed the data on their own and then compared their analyses. And then they analyzed the other data together and discussed how to either choose or ignore the data. After several deliberations, they finally reached an agreement.

The first step was the screening of participants. At the inception of this step, ten teachers from one school were identified as participant candidates. Participant candidates were selected according to their willing and interest. Then the researcher characterized the ten participant candidates' theoretical beliefs. The researcher asked the participants to finish two tasks, which were the statement survey of beliefs inventory and the lesson plan selection. The result was used to select the four participants to participate in the study while considering their ages and characteristics in EFL teaching together.

The second step of the study was data collection through interviews and classroom observation. At first, a pre-interview of those case teachers was conducted to collect their background information and the teachers' beliefs about English, which could be used as the materials introducing each participant case. Then, another semi-structured interview was to investigate teachers' attitudes towards giving correction to students' errors. Next was micro observation for each teacher (three lessons per teacher) . After that, the researcher gave the participants an explanation aiming to introduce the six categories of corrective feedback after each person's three lessons. Simultaneously, follow-up interviews were conducted with the individual participants to investigate their beliefs about CF.

The third step was to analyze data and compare results. After data analysis and comparison, the final interview was conducted to fulfill the data. Detailed findings from the four selected cases were presented and discussed in the next chapter. Data from interviews with participants, checklist of the observed lessons, and transcribed classroom extracts were analyzed from a qualitative perspective. Informal talks with teachers and the individual interviews with the participants were analyzed to help get better understanding of the participants' performance and perceptions. Data of each teacher participant's three classroom observations were used to discern EFL teachers' real-life CF practices. After gaining the teacher participants' beliefs and practices about CF, the researcher compared the two kinds of data and found out the answer to the third research question, which was to what extent the EFL teachers' beliefs about CF were congruent with their observed teaching practices.

CHAPTER 4

RESULTS AND DISCUSSION

4

Introduction

The purpose of this chapter is to provide the study's results of teachers' beliefs and practices about corrective feedback. This chapter presents the case studies of the four participating teachers at Yucai No.3 Primary School in the city of Shenzhen. The four teachers are identified by their English names (Ida, Vincent, Claire and Jane) to ensure confidentiality. All the four case studies include coded data from classroom observations and transcribed data from both interviews and observations.

The researcher and the second researcher interviewed the four participants and observed their classrooms from April to July, 2014. Twelve lessons were observed, and all the lessons were video recorded and data collected. Each teacher participant showed two well-prepared lessons called open classes and one common lesson. Before each observation, the researchers and the participants would informally talk about the lessons and the teaching plans briefly in order to gain some information before being observed. The researcher with the help of the second researcher transcribed the data as soon as each class ended in order to ensure the accuracy and validity of transcription (see Appendix 8 Observation Checklist of Teachers' CF) .

Teachers can hold beliefs unconsciously and teachers may not be able to express these beliefs or may be unwilling to express any unpopular belief, and they may prefer to state socially desirable beliefs（Kagan, 1990）. Therefore, it is preferable to access beliefs indirectly. For these reasons, the researcher used four semi-structured interviews to collect data about teachers' beliefs, in which teachers were asked to recount specific cases and anecdotes（Kagan, 1990; Woods, 1996; Gass & Mackey, 2000）. The interviews aimed to enquire beliefs in the abstract about teachers' orientations towards English teaching and giving corrective feedback in daily teaching and their interactive thinking and decision making on CF use.

Each teacher's stated beliefs about English teaching and CF and their classroom practices were considered in turn. The teachers are listed in order of their teaching experience, beginning with the least experienced teacher to the most experienced one. Each case study of the participants will be examined from the framework of the stated research questions. This chapter is organized as follows. The first section presents each participant's introduction, beliefs about CF, classroom practices about CF, and comparison between beliefs and practices. The second section presents a cross-case analysis. Finally, a brief summary shows the factors affecting teachers' CF practices.

Case Studies

Case study 1: Ida

1. Introducing Ida

Ida was born in Shandong Province. She graduated from a very famous university called Xinan University and she received her Master degree in English. She is 27 years old and the youngest of the four teacher participants involved. She has three years of teaching experience. Her students are in their second year of primary school. Ida is a teacher who is very patient and generous to students. She would like to offer sufficient opportunities to her students in her EFL classes. Although she only has three years' teaching experience, she has become a popular teacher among her students and has a very good reputation with her students' parents. It's quite obvious that the school leaders treat Ida as a promising young teacher.

Ida described an ideal EFL classroom in her eyes in this way: Students would be active in thinking and the teacher would lead the class effectively. The classroom would have a pleasant atmosphere. Students would talk actively and even argue in English, and the teacher would give additional information to the students. Both the teacher and the students would be very happy and the class would be enjoyable for all the class members. All Ida's descriptions of an ideal EFL classroom reveal that she is trying her best to be a great EFL teacher and make her students learn English as efficiently as possible.

Ida recalled that when she was a student, she read a plethora of English articles loudly. When she became an English teacher, she used this learning method to teach her students and encouraged them to open their mouths to read and talk aloud. She also thought that her teaching beliefs came from experienced teachers and books. Ida said that she gave lessons as she planned but changed them a little depending on the class and execution of the lesson. She also often designed student-centered activities. Her main focus was on the fluency of students' spoken English. She was confident to say that her teaching beliefs and her teaching practices could be matched with each other. From what Ida said, we can get the information that her teaching beliefs are from many aspects, her personal learning experiences and her schooling, and even random training from her colleague teachers and so on, which shows us that Ida is a studious young teacher.

2. Ida's beliefs about CF

The researcher made a qualitative analysis of the four interview data from Ida. The results of the semi-structured interview data are summarized below based on four themes that outline Ida's beliefs about CF.

Attitude towards Giving Students the Correction of Errors

The second interview (see Appendix 5) was employed in an attempt to view the findings of teacher participants' attitude towards giving students the correction of errors. The interview contained nine semi-structured questions on teachers' beliefs about CF. From Ida's answers to the nine semi-structured questions we can summarize her main viewpoints as below.

Ida strongly agrees that making errors is natural. She agrees with the following viewpoints: ①immediate correction is good for students' learning; ②teacher correction is generally effective; ③it's hard for students to notice their own errors; ④all errors in writing must be corrected; ⑤individual correction of errors in writing is useful. Ida disagrees that all errors in speaking must be corrected. She is not sure if correction of oral errors in class undermines the learner's self-esteem, or if peer feedback is beneficial. When asked about her reasons, she explained:

I think that the immediate correction plays an important role in language learning, especially in writing. On the one hand, it helps learners understand the writing rules or grammars of foreign languages and even their own mother language. On the other hand, the immediate correction of all oral errors may lead to the interruption of students' thinking, which may undermine the learners' confidence of oral expressions. The fluency of speaking, representing the fluency of the thinking, is more important than the accuracy in the foreign language learning.

(Ida, the second interview, April, 2014)

Ida's explanation reveals that she has clear ideas about correcting students' errors both in oral or written practices. She has her own understanding of when, how and why to correct her students' errors, and when to ignore her students' errors.

The Foci of CF

Ida considered CF as an important part of instruction for students from teachers when she was learning English. CF would help students have good habits of expression and a correct language sense in English. Ida viewed herself as a teacher who often used CF in her English classroom. She had such an idea that it was a process with lots of errors continually for low graders in primary school to learn English well. When giving students CF, Ida said she would keep students' pride and self-confidence in mind. She would try her best not to hurt her students' pride, or to embarrass them. She would pay attention to students' learning reaction and interests. Sometimes she would not correct students' errors temporarily in order not to influence their learning interests and emotion. Moreover, Ida thought:

As a teacher I have to pay attention to the whole interests of the big size of the class, instead of sticking to one student's errors.

(Ida, the third interview, June, 2014)

She was very sure that she had the teaching concept that let some students grasp the key knowledge and the others follow up with the help of the advanced fellow classmates. Ida thought that the foci of CF would be the pronunciation errors and the frequently existing errors. Her reasons were like these: Pronunciation is very important for primary school students, especially the low graders. The frequently existing errors are the barriers of English learning. Nevertheless, she would always adopt measures of ignoring the errors when students were expressing their ideas in a long passage. At that moment, comprehension came first.

Beliefs about What Types of CF Should be Focus on

Ida preferred to use these three types of CF: recast, elicitation and repetition for the sake of protecting students, making students understand easily, and quickly noticing their errors. The three types of CF Ida chose also helped her save time in class, because the teaching contents were excessive most of the time, as she often gave students more materials to learn for the purpose of helping students learn more every term. Ida analyzed the other three types of CF in this way:

I think that metalinguistic feedback and clarification request are not euphemistic and too burdensome. Explicit correction is the most straight one, but it is one CF which is easy to discourage students' learning enthusiasm.

(Ida, the second interview, April, 2014)

So Ida preferred to use these three types of CF: recast, elicitation and repetition. And according to her expression and explanation, we can see that she has deep thinking about the six types of CF (Lyster and Ranta, 1997) after the researcher's explanation of their characteristics.

Overall Impression on CF

In terms of corrective feedback, Ida tended to be more meaning-focused. Before the training of corrective feedback, Ida was not sure about the technical term CF, but she was doing it in all her classes. Ida thought that teachers' CF helped students improve their English efficiently. She had two reasons for this: First, the teacher corrected one student's errors, which would influence the whole class. Second, when the teacher noticed the students' common errors, she would ask the whole class to pay attention to them and repeat the correct ones together and all made progress. Ida said that her students repeated at once every time when she gave CF to them, but most of the time, they could not remember the correction of their errors the next day. So repeating the correction of the errors was very important and necessary.

3. Ida's classroom practices on CF

Ida teaches three classes in Grade Two, which consists of 50 students in each class. The students have just less than two years of English learning experience. Most of them are very active and dedicated in Ida's classes. The class atmosphere is very relaxed and comfortable. Many of the students said that they felt time flies in Ida's classes. Ida's classes that have been observed are "Unit 9, My clothes" "Unit 10, Activities", and "Unit 12, A girl and three bears" and the time is between May and June, 2014. The results of the classroom observations are summarized below based on two themes that outline Ida's CF practices. Theme One: The types of CF Ida focused on. Theme Two: The foci of CF in Ida's classroom practices.

In terms of the amount of CF, Ida provided 19 instances of CF during the three lessons. As shown in Table 5, the details of CF types used and the percentage of each CF type used compared to the total amount of CF used are all very obvious in the table.

Table 5 The observation checklist result of Ida's three observed classes

Types of CF	Ida's three classes
Explicit correction	1 (5.2%)
Recast	14 (74%)
Elicitation	1 (5.2%)
Metalinguistic feedback	1 (5.2%)

续 表

Types of CF	Ida's three classes
Clarification request	1（5.2%）
Repetition	1（5.2%）

Considering linguistic targets of CF, Table 6 shows that Ida's CF focused mainly on students' grammar errors（58%）, followed by CF of pronunciation errors（21%）and CF of vocabulary errors（21%）, respectively.

Table 6 Ida's CF on linguistic targets of errors in her three observed classes

Grammar	Vocabulary	Pronunciation
11（58%）	4（21%）	4（21%）

From Table 6, we can find that the most common type of Ida's CF in the three classes is recast. The results show that recast is the type of CF that leads to the highest percentage 74%, which accounts for more than one half in the entire proportion. Recast has the dominant position in Ida's feedback types in her EFL classroom practices.

Ida's Classroom Episode 1（Grammar）（Recast）:

T：If it is rainy, what would you do?

S：I am in home and play computer games.

T：I am at home and play computer games.

（Ida, observation, June, 2014）

In Ida's Classroom Episode 1, the students make an error on the linguistic target named grammar（Lyster, 1998）, and then Ida provides the reformulation by recast. The student then notices the error at once and makes the correction by means of repetition. Although repetition cannot be considered as the student absolutely gains uptake or acquisition of the correction of his error, it at least manifests that the student notices the referred form. Only when the student notices the difference between his own saying and the supplied target-like correction can recast finally take effect (Ellis, Loewen and Erlam, 2006). Ida noticed that it was not easy for the students to remember the correct forms of their errors given by the teacher, so she told the researcher in the third interview that: Repetition of the same errors' CF is essential for students' EFL learning.

Ida's Classroom Episode 2 (Vocabulary) (Recast):

S1: What else do you need?

S2: I have a new T-shirt.

T: Need.

S2: I need a new T-shirt.

(Ida, observation, May, 2014)

Ida recasts the student's vocabulary error of the linguistic targets in her Classroom Episode 2, and the student quickly responds to her feedback by reforming the sentence with the correct word given. The student's reforming performance proves that he comprehends his teacher's intention at once.

Ida's Classroom Episode 3 (Pronunciation) (Clarification request):

S: It's sunny. Let's go to "Baris".

T: Pardon?

S: "Baris".

T: Paris.

(Ida, observation, June, 2014)

In Ida's Classroom Episode 3, she uses the CF type clarification request to correct her student's pronunciation error. When she uses "pardon" aiming to remind the student to think over the utterance again and get the correct saying, but her student still keeps on saying the wrong pronunciation.Then Ida gives the correct pronunciation directly, and instead of waiting for a reaction from the student, Ida continues her lesson without any pause. All these reveal apparently that Ida does not recognize such a problem that the teacher's handling method on CF should also be taken into account for students' reaction.

4. Comparison between Ida's beliefs and practices

After the data collection and analysis of semi-structured interviews and classroom observations, the researcher examined the observational data with the help of the second researcher to identify how often Ida's CF practices were initiated in her beliefs about CF.

In relating Ida's beliefs to observational data, the researcher did not want to simply confirm or deny whether Ida's beliefs were evident in her practices. As Lu Liu（2003: 47）stated: "No one should expect that teachers' beliefs are either always contradictory to his or her practices or in accordance with his or her practices." The main purpose of this study is to find out to what extent teachers' beliefs are congruent with their practices. To be more clear, the researcher will also show the instances which are about teachers' beliefs incongruent with their practices.

Ida's beliefs about CF incongruent with her classroom practices

The inconsistency between Ida's beliefs about CF and her observed practices will be shown in three points:

1. Ida thought that the foci of CF would be the pronunciation errors and the frequently existing errors. Yet in her three observed lessons, she paid more attention to the linguistic target grammar（58%）, pronunciation and vocabulary both came next（21%）.

2. Although Ida indicated that she preferred to use these three types of CF: recast, elicitation and repetition for the sake of protecting students, making the students understand easily, and quickly noticing their errors. In her observed classes, recast was the type of CF that led to the highest percentage（74%）. We can only

find one elicitation (5.2%) and one repetition (5.2%) among all her 19 samples of CF.

3. Ida disagreed that all errors in speaking must be corrected. Sometimes she would neglect students' errors temporarily in order not to influence their learning interests and emotion. She would always adopt measures of ignoring the errors when students were expressing their ideas in a long passage. From the observed classes, it was quite obvious that Ida paid attention to almost all her students' errors and gave CF to all the errors (See Appendix 7).

Ida's beliefs about CF congruent with her classroom practices

The consistency between Ida's beliefs about CF and her observed practices will be shown in several points:

1. When giving students CF, Ida said she would keep students' pride and self-confidence in mind. She would try her best not to hurt her students' pride, or embarrass them. From Ida's observed classes, we can see that she actually followed what she said. Her students acted confidently in her class and they did not feel nervous to make errors. All this comes from Ida's kindness and care to the students.

2. Ida believed herself to be a teacher who often used CF in her English classroom. Obviously, yes, Ida tried her best to give CF in her classes. She was very sensitive to students' errors and gave CF immediately in her observed three classes.

3. Ida analyzed these three types of CF in this way: Metalinguistic feedback and clarification request are not euphemistic and too burdensome. Explicit correction is the most straight one, but it is one CF which is easy to discourage students' learning enthusiasm. Ida's classroom practices were consistent with her beliefs. Among her total 19 CF in her three observed classes, she only had one metalinguistic feedback (5.2%), one clarification request (5.2%) and one explicit correction (5.2%).

Case study 2: Vincent

1. Introducing Vincent

Vincent was born in Hubei Province. He graduated from a college called Shashi

University and he got his college degree of English Major there. He is 33 years old. He has ten years of teaching experience. His students are in their fifth year of primary school. Vincent is very humorous and kind to his students. So he is very popular among them.

Vincent described his ideal EFL classroom in his eyes in this way: Students would use English fluently and directly in meaningful communicative activities and problem-solving in English classes. They would catch every occasion and opportunity to talk in English and have great motivation to show their ideas in the way of English thinking.

Vincent said that his own experience of language learning was from his education school and his self-study, for example, reading English stories, watching English movies, and listening to English songs. He thought that his own language learning experience had a great influence on the way he taught. He stated that English songs, movies and cultures often permeated his classes. He thought that his beliefs in his teaching stemmed from his own daily teaching and he would change to some extent according to the feedback from the students he taught before, which meant that Vincent kept in close touch with the students he taught and often talked with them to get some feedback about his teaching. Vincent said that he often gave his lessons according to the actual situation, for instance, the classroom atmosphere, students' learning desires, students' learning difficulties, and so on. Instead of basing on his teaching plan, for example, when he gave the students revision lessons, he would develop his lesson closely according to the students' emotional and learning state. He also thought that he often designed student-centered activities. He paid more attention to the fluency of students' spoken English and the accuracy of students' homework. Vincent didn't think his teaching beliefs and his teaching practices could be matched with each other. He stated that the factors that hindered the matching were several aspects, including students' learning state, students' cultural understanding (He gave a recall that his students did not understand an interesting Western joke given by him.) and not clearly knowing students' knowledge reserve.

2. Vincent's beliefs about CF

The researcher made an analysis of the four semi-structured interview data from Vincent. The results are summarized below based on four themes that outline Vincent's beliefs about CF.

Attitude towards Giving Students the Correction of Errors

Vincent strongly agrees that making errors is natural and that teachers' correction is generally effective, and that individual correction of errors in writing is useful. He agrees with the following viewpoints: ①immediate correction is good for students' learning; ②it's hard for students to notice their own errors; ③all errors in writing must be corrected; ④correction of oral errors in the class undermines the learner's self-esteem; ⑤peer feedback is beneficial. Vincent strongly disagrees that all errors in speaking must be corrected. Vincent adds an explanation for this:

It is true that giving students the correction of errors would sometimes embarrass and discourage students, and teachers' frequent error correction action does not seem to help students learn anything. Such a situation often happens in our daily teaching as we teachers try our best to correct students' errors, yet they keep on making the same errors. I don't think there is a single answer to the question of exactly how teachers should correct students' errors because I think that error correction is more of an art than a science, which requires teachers to make a quick judgment while considering many different factors.

(Vincent, the second interview, April, 2014)

Vincent treats error correction as an art instead of a science, which shows us that he has deep thinking on this point. He is smart and flexible in his EFL daily teaching. He knows and understands that what he always faces are children, lovely and clever children. Each child is special, and every class has its own characteristics. So, the teacher needs to treat the errors according to the real situation and make the appropriate response. What is to be summed up is that Vincent's attitude towards error correction is based on the real situation in front of him instead of unalterable choices.

The Foci of CF

Vincent stated that corrective feedback was very important in his English class. He explained that giving CF was for the purpose of giving students a correct guide and helping them have good English expression habits. CF has the effect or function of guiding and demonstrating. Vincent indicated that he did not often use CF in his class, because too much CF would result in students losing their confidence. However, the outstanding students could be given more CF, because they are more confident most of the time. When giving students CF, Vincent would care about students' self-esteem, especially the poor students. When asked about the foci of CF, Vincent said that the foci were the unit's emphasis points and the difficult learning points. He explained that the purpose was to help students learn the main knowledge points of the unit. Vincent considered that it was unnecessary to have CF when students were having oral communication. He added his reasons below:

Even when we talk in our mother tongue Chinese, it's normal to make errors, so errors are natural. When students are practicing their oral English, the most important thing is that they dare to open their mouths and have confidence to communicate with others. Encouragement is the only thing the teacher should do at the moment.

(Vincent, the third interview, June, 2014)

According to Vincent's words, it's quite easy to know that he is a teacher who is good at encouraging students and he pays more attention to students' confidence and fluency instead of accuracy when students are having oral communication. Vincent's foci of CF are referring each unit's emphasis points and the difficult learning points, mostly refer to grammar.

Beliefs about What Types of CF Should Be Focus on

Vincent stated that he used two types of CF in his classes: elicitation and clarification request. He thought that these two types of CF were suitable for primary students. They would help students to think. Vincent also said that the types of CF to be focused on were based on his own habits, or based on the situation of the classes he was teaching at the moment. He also said that maybe he would like to use two types of CF in one type of error correction. He added the explanation that he was always teaching according to the actual situation in the real-life classroom. He also said that teaching must always be flexible.

Overall Impression on CF

Vincent expressed that he was more form-focused when he taught students how to write, and he was more meaning-focused when in the English speaking class. Before the training of corrective feedback, Vincent was not sure about the technical term CF, but he was using it in all his classes. When asked for his idea about whether teachers' CF helped students improve their English learning or not, Vincent answered yes without any hesitation, and he also added information that this was the case both in oral or writing teaching. He was very sure that students accepted the CF given by him. But repeating the CF of the errors was necessary and important.

3. Vincent's classroom practices on CF

Vincent teaches two classes of Grade five, which consists of 50 students in each class. He is also one class master (a teacher in charge of the class) . The researcher and the second researcher observed Vincent three lessons between May and June, 2014. The topics of Vincent's classes that have been observed are "Typhoon" "Sports Day", and "Stories enjoying". The results of the classroom observations are summarized below based on two main themes that outline Vincent's CF practices. Theme One: The Types of CF that Vincent focused on. Theme Two: The foci of CF in Vincent's classroom practices.

In terms of the amount of CF, Vincent provided 17 instances of CF during the three lessons. As shown in Table 7, the details of types of CF used and the percentages are all very obvious in the table. The most common type of Vincent's CF in the three classes is recast. The results show that recast is the type of CF that leads to the highest percentage, which is 27%, and followed by explicit correction（20%）and repetition（20%）, respectively.

Table 7　The observation checklist result of Vincent's three observed classes

Types of CF	Vincent's three classes
Explicit correction	3（20%）
Recast	4（27%）
Elicitation	2（13%）
Metalinguistic feedback	2（13%）
Clarification request	1（7%）
Repetition	3（20%）

Considering linguistic targets of CF, Table 8 shows that Vincent's CF focused mainly on students' grammar errors（67%）, followed by vocabulary errors CF（20%）and finally pronunciation errors CF（13%）.

Table 8　Number and linguistic targets of Vincent's CF in his three observed classes

Grammar	Vocabulary	Pronunciation
10（67%）	3（20%）	2（13%）

Vincent likes to use two types of CF at one time. When asked the reason for this, he said that he wanted to help his students be more clear about their errors and understand the knowledge key points, and also help students be active in thinking. For example, he gave CF repetition first, and then explicit correction came next in one specific error correcting instance, as seen below:

Vincent's Classroom Episode 1 (Vocabulary) (Repetition & Explicit correction) :

S: I can play football. I can high jump.

T: I can high jump?

S: I can play the high jump.

T: No, do.

S: I can do the high jump.

(Vincent, observation, June, 2014)

In Vincent' s Classroom Episode 1, he uses repetition to ask his student to pay attention to the sentence "I can high jump." . And the student realizes his error and tries his best to correct it by himself. But the student' s self-correction is not correct. At that moment, Vincent used explicit correction to give CF to the student. When the researcher asked Vincent why he made this decision, he said that the student had his own understanding, which meant that the student had deep thinking and had his own distinctive opinions.

For using two different types of error correction he responded by stating that he had two reasons: Firstly, I want to draw my students' attention by changing different strategies. Secondly, the time is limited in one lesson, and I cannot stick to one student's one error and spend so much time on it. I have to care for other students.

(Vincent, the fourth interview, July, 2014)

Vincent's Classroom Episode 2 (Grammar) (Explicit correction & Metalinguistic feedback) :

S: Putted.

T: No, put—put, read—read, cut—cut, hit—hit.

(Vincent, observation, May, 2014)

From Vincent's above Classroom Episode 2, we can see that he makes his students understand clearly about the knowledge point. He wants his students to draw inferences about other cases from one instance.

Vincent's Classroom Episode 3 (Vocabulary) (Recast):

S: I can't ball.

T: Throw a ball.

S: I can't throw a ball.

(Vincent, observation, June, 2014)

Vincent's Classroom Episode 4 (Vocabulary & Grammar) (Elicitation):

S1: When time for dinner?

T: Any errors?

S2: What time for dinner?

T: Any other answer?

S3: When's Anna's dinner?

T: What time... When...

(Vincent, observation, June, 2014)

Vincent's Classroom Episode 5 (Pronunciation) (Repetition):

S: I can play "footer-ball".

T: "Footer-ball"?

(Students laugh.)

T: Say after me—football, basketball, table tennis.

(Vincent, observation, June, 2014)

In Vincent's Classroom Episode 3, 4, and 5, he shows his desire to help his students learn the correct English. Vincent uses different CF to draw his students' attention to the errors when he realizes that students have made the same errors frequently. He keeps on giving CF without losing patience. It is proved by Mackey and Philp's assertion (1998) that feedback to the errors of often occurring linguistic features more apt to trigger changes in learners' language output than that directed at the errors of infrequently occurring linguistic form.

4. Comparison between Vincent's beliefs and practices

The researcher made a qualitative analysis of Vincent's four interview data and three classroom observations with the help of the second researcher. Afterwards, the researcher examined the observational data to identify how often Vincent's CF practices were initiated in his beliefs about CF. The main purpose is to find out to what extent Vincent's beliefs are congruent with his practices. To be more clear, the researcher will also show the instances where Vincent's beliefs are incongruent with his practices.

Vincent's beliefs about CF are incongruent with his classroom practices

The inconsistency between Vincent's beliefs about CF and his observed practices will be shown in several points:

Vincent considered that it was unnecessary to have CF when students were having oral communication. According to his three classes, Vincent gave CF when students were having oral communication in fact. For example, when four students were having group communication, Vincent stopped them and gave CF as seen below:

Vincent's Classroom Episode 6 (Grammar) (Explicit correction):

S1: What is Bob going to do?

S2: Bob is going to running.

S3: What's Tim going to do?

S4: He is do the high jump.

T: He is going to run, not running. "Be going to". He is going to do the high jump.

(Vincent, observation, June, 2014)

Vincent stated that he used two types of CF in his classes：elicitation and clarification request. Actually, in Vincent's three observed classes, he only used two elicitations and one clarification request. The ones of CF he used more were recast, repetition and explicit correction.

Vincent's beliefs about CF are congruent with his classroom practices

The consistency between Vincent's beliefs about CF and his observed practices will be shown in several points：

1. Vincent indicated that he did not often use CF in his class, because too much CF would result in students losing confidence. According to Vincent's observational data, he actually ignored some students' errors. Two instances can be seen below.

Vincent's Classroom Episode 7（Grammar）：

S1：Miss Li give Anna a bike. Is Anna happy?

（Vincent, observation, June, 2014）

Vincent just paid attention to the key sentence "Is Anna happy?". He didn't give any CF to the error of S1's first sentence " Miss Li give Anna a bike.". He told the researcher that this student could give the key sentence correctly, which meant that he made big progress. Vincent wanted the student to be more confident.

Vincent's Classroom Episode 8（Grammar）：

S2：Who is they new friend?

（Vincent, observation, June, 2014）

Vincent didn't give CF to change "they" to "their". His reason was that it was great progress for this student to say out the key word phrase "new friend". He also added that to help a student have confidence, the most useful measure was to encourage him or her often.

2. When asked about the foci of CF, Vincent said that the foci were the unit's emphasis points and the difficult points. He really paid almost all his attention to the unit's emphasis points and the difficult points during his actual classroom practices.

3. Vincent was confident that he taught EFL in a flexible way, and especially when he gave CF to students, he would like to use two types of CF in one type of error correction. And he treated the actual situation as his basis of CF types choosing. According to Vincent's classroom observation data, he used two types of CF in one time often and he was in fact a teacher who gave CF to his students flexibly.

Case study 3: Claire

1. Introducing Claire

Claire was born in Hunan Province. She graduated from a college called Yueyang Normal College and she received her college degree of English Education there. She is 36 years old. She has 14 years of teaching experience. Her students are in Grades Two and Five.

Claire described her ideal EFL classroom in this way: The teacher creates the class situation for the students. The students try their best to communicate with each other and study independently and get into the swing of their learning.

When talking about English learning experience, Claire stated that she learned English in two main ways, which were through school English lessons when she was at school and by watching movies. She thought her own language learning experience influenced the way she taught. She holds the view that her belief in her teaching was mainly from her experienced colleagues. She gave her lessons based on the actual classroom situation most of the time. She often designed student-centered activities. When asked, she said she paid more attention to students' spoken English than their written English. She also said that when she taught Grade One and Two students, she paid more attention to the fluency of spoken English. And when she taught Grade Three to Six students, she paid the same attention to both students' spoken and written

English. Claire is very confident that her teaching beliefs and her teaching practices are matched.

2. Claire's beliefs about CF

The results of the four semi-structured interview data are summarized below based on four themes that outline Claire's beliefs about CF.

Attitude towards Giving Students the Correction of Errors

Claire strongly agrees that making errors is natural. She strongly disagrees that all errors in speaking must be corrected.

She agrees with the following viewpoints：①it's hard for students to notice their own errors; ②correction of oral errors in class undermines the learner's self-esteem; ③individual correction of errors in writing is useful; ④peer feedback is beneficial.

She is not sure about these viewpoints: ①immediate correction is good for students' learning; ②teacher correction is generally effective; ③all errors in writing must be corrected. Claire's statement shows her attitude as below：

In a word, choosing CF should be based on the teaching content and the teaching situation. Giving CF should not undermine students' learning initiative. However, teachers should lead students to have correct English language speaking and writing habits.

（Claire, the second interview, April, 2014）

The Foci of CF

Claire considered CF to be an important part of the English class. She explained that CF helped students notice their errors and get the right answer timely and learn English well. Claire thought that she used CF frequently in her classes. When she was giving students CF, she worried about undermining students' learning enthusiasm, especially sensitive students. Therefore, she preferred to ask fellow students to help each other find out errors and correct them by themselves. Claire stated that she would use more CF when students were learning important sentence patterns. She used more CF in new lesson presentation and exercise lessons. She would neglect students' errors when it was their show time.

Beliefs about What Types of CF Should be Focus on

Claire stated that she used all the six types of CF in her classes: explicit correction, recast, elicitation, metalinguistic feedback, clarification request and repetition. When the researcher asked her to think about it more carefully, she added that although she liked all the types of CF, what she often used and liked better were recast and repetition. She explained that she liked to be more euphemistic when she was giving students CF.

Overall Impression on CF

Claire was very sure that she was more meaning-focused when she gave CF to students. Before the training of corrective feedback, she was not sure about the technical term CF, but she was using it in all her classes. Claire was certain that teachers' CF helped students improve their English learning efficiently. Most students would change their common errors when they heard their teacher's correction of the errors, and then they would repeat after the teacher vocally or silently. When talking about how students dealt with the corrective feedback given by the teacher, Claire was not very sure. She showed two main parts of students: some were nervous and became disruptive, while others might remember the correction of the errors.

3. Claire's classroom practices on CF

Claire teaches two classes in Grade Five and one class in Grade Two, consisting of 50 students in each class. The first and the second researchers observed Claire's three lessons between May and June, 2014. Claire's classes that were observed are "Summer holidays" "I'm Danny", and "A School Outing". The results of the classroom observations are summarized below based on the two themes that outline

Claire's CF practices. Theme One: The types of CF that Claire focused on. Theme Two: The foci of CF in Claire's classroom practices.

In terms of the amount of CF, Claire provided twelve instances of CF during the three lessons. As shown in Table 9, the details of CF types used and the percentages are all shown in the table. We can find that the most common type of Claire's CF in the three classes is recast. The results show that recast is the type of CF that leads to the highest percentage, which is 75%, and two types of other CF, which are two elicitations（17%）and one repetition（8%）.

Table 9 The observation checklist result of Claire's three observed classes

Types of CF	Claire's three classes
Explicit correction	0
Recast	9（75%）
Elicitation	2（17%）
Metalinguistic feedback	0
Clarification request	0
Repetition	1（8%）

From the table above, we can figure out that Claire only used three types of CF. According to the observational data, we find that Claire neglected students' errors sometimes, even the errors that happened frequently. One example will be shown below.

Claire's Classroom Episode 1

S: You are girl.

（Claire, observation, June, 2014）

Claire's students frequently had the above Episode 1's error, but she paid no attention to it. She just encouraged her students to keep on talking and she was very happy when her students were brave to stand up and speak English loudly. Claire showed her perspective of her neglecting students' errors.

My students' English levels are not so good. And they are not very confident to open their mouths and talk often. So I keep on encouraging them to speak. Sometimes I try not to pay any attention to some of their errors. For example, my student said that "You are girl." not "You are a girl.". I think it's not a big error and everyone can understand. So I decided to ignore it.

(Claire, the fourth interview, July, 2014)

Considering linguistic targets of CF, Table 10 shows that Claire's CF focused mainly on students' grammar errors (50%) , followed by vocabulary error CF (33%) and pronunciation error CF (17%) .

Table 10 Number and linguistic targets of Claire's CF in her three observed classes

Grammar	Vocabulary	Pronunciation
6 (50%)	4 (33%)	2 (17%)

Some of Claire's CF classroom episodes are shown below to help understand her real classroom practices.

Claire's Classroom Episode 2 (Grammar) (Recast) :

S: I am a short.

T: I am short.

(Claire, observation, June, 2014)

Claire recasts her student's error in her Classroom Episode 2. When talking about recast in the fourth interview, she argues that recast can eliminate the risk of hurting students' confidence and interests, which is consistent with the commonly accepted views.

Claire's Classroom Episode 3（Vocabulary）（Elicitation）:

S1: The children are very hot.

T: The children are very ..., no water.

Ss: Thirsty.

T: Yes, thirsty. The children are very thirsty.

（Claire, observation, June, 2014）

The common strategies for eliciting are constituted by questioning, pausing skillfully for students to complete or filling in the oral discourse（Lyster and Ranta, 1997）. In Claire's Classroom Episode 3, she urges her students to think and choose one adjective to complete her sentence. And the students finally meet her expectation by choosing the modification.

Claire's Classroom Episode 4（Pronunciation）（Repetition）:

S: I read / riː d / a book last night.

T: Read / riː d /?

S: I read / red / a book last night.

（Claire, observation, May, 2014）

A repetition usually means that the teacher repeats the problematic part of students' utterance（Lyster and Ranta, 1997）. In Claire's Classroom Episode 4, she repeats the erroneous part of the student's pronunciation linguistic target with intentional rising pitch and stress, which is supposed to remind the student of the error. And the student understands Claire and uptakes the right pronunciation.

4. Comparison between Claire's beliefs and practices

The researcher made a qualitative analysis of Claire's four interview data and three classroom observations with the help of the second researcher. Then, the researcher examined the observational data to identify how often Claire's CF practices were initiated in her beliefs about CF. Doing all this is to find out to what extent Claire's beliefs are congruent with her practices. To be more clear, the researcher will also show the instances where Claire's beliefs incongruent with her practices.

Claire's beliefs about CF are incongruent with her classroom practices

The inconsistency between Claire's beliefs about CF and her observed practices will be shown in two points:

1. Claire thought that she used CF frequently in her classes. Actually, she did not often use CF in her three observed classes. When the researcher told her the observation result, she was surprised. She claimed that the teaching contents of these three observed classes were not difficult.

Maybe the contents of these three lessons were quite simple, and the students made good preview beforehand. So, they made fewer errors. Then there was not so much CF.

(Claire, the fourth interview, July, 2014)

2. Claire stated that she used all the six types of CF in her classes: explicit correction, recast, elicitation, metalinguistic feedback, clarification request and repetition. She confirmed that although she liked all the types of CF, what she often used and liked better were recast and repetition. Claire's beliefs were not congruent with her practices. She only used three types of CF. Although she emphasized recast and repetition, she only used one repetition in her observed classes.

Claire's beliefs about CF are congruent with her classroom practices

The consistency between Claire's beliefs about CF and her observed practices will be shown in three points:

1. Claire strongly disagreed that all errors in speaking must be corrected. In fact, she did not correct all her students' spoken errors.

2. Claire stated that she would use more CF when students were learning the important sentence patterns. Actually, she stuck to the important sentence patterns of her teaching plans closely according to the classes the researcher observed. She gave CF when students had errors in practicing the key sentence patterns.

3. Claire would neglect students' errors when it was their English show time. Yes, she did it in her classroom practices.

Case study 4: Jane

1. Introducing Jane

Jane was born in Hunan Province. She graduated from a college called Yiyang Normal College and she got her college degree in English Education there. Several years later after her graduation, she received her English bachelor degree of Zhongnan University through self-study. She is the oldest one among the four teacher participants. She is 43 years old. She has 21 years of teaching experience. Her students are in Grades Three and Four.

Jane described her ideal EFL classroom in her eyes this way: The teacher and the students should have a harmonious relationship. The students should be actively engaged in class. And the teacher's direction and teaching should be highly efficient. Both the teacher and the students would be very happy and all the activities would be in good order.

Jane talked about her own experience of language teaching in a reflective way. When she was in high school, her English teacher paid a lot of attention to grammar. When she was in college, her focus centered on English vocabulary, grammar, speaking, and especially reading, and these were all developed together. She thought that her own language learning experience had a significant influence on the way she taught. Jane stated the sources of her teaching beliefs this way: her teachers' influence, learning from other colleague teachers, and the experience gained from interaction with other students. Most of the time, Jane delivered her lessons as she planned them. Sometimes she based these lessons on the actual situation, because each class had its own special dynamic character because of the different students with different abilities. Jane often designed student-centered activities having students often work in pairs or in small groups. Jane paid more attention to students' spoken English and fluency when she taught Grades One to Three. She paid more attention to students' written English and accuracy when she taught students from Grades Four to Six. When asked whether her teaching beliefs and teaching practice were matched with each other or not, her answer was that sometimes they were not. What prevented this from happening involved many factors, such as too many students in the class or different levels of students in a class.

2. Jane's beliefs about CF

The results of the interview data are summarized below based on four themes that outline Jane's beliefs about CF.

Attitude towards Giving Students the Correction of Errors

Jane strongly agrees with the following five points: ①making errors is natural; ②it's hard for students to notice their own errors; ③all errors in writing must be corrected; ④individual correction of errors in writing is useful; ⑤peer feedback is beneficial. She strongly disagrees that all errors in speaking must be corrected. She disagrees that correction of oral errors in the class undermines the learner's self-esteem.

She agrees with the following two points: ①immediate correction is good for students' learning; ②teacher correction is generally effective.

As long as students are learning, it's natural for them to have errors. If students have no errors during their learning, then they don't need to learn any more, or we can say that they have grasped all the learning content. However, when students are learning a new language point, it's unavoidable for them to have different kinds of errors during their learning process, especially when they are learning the difficult grammar points. I think it's hard for students to notice their own errors. So I often ask my students to practice the exercises of errors correcting. Most of the time, students are enlightened suddenly when the teacher or other students point out the errors in the exercises. So, I am always ready to give CF when my students have one kind of error for the first time. I don't want my students to have fossilization because of their errors. So, immediate correction is very important for students' EFL learning. Nevertheless, errors in spoken English cannot all be corrected whenever discovered. Frequent CF for spoken English may result in students losing confidence to continue talking and even hurt their pride. So, I would neglect my students' errors when their expression can be understood in communication.

(Jane, the second interview, April, 2014)

The Foci of CF

Jane stated that CF was important for students' English learning. She explained that if teachers did not give students CF, then their errors would always be errors and sometime later, the errors might be fossilized, or habitual, or even students would accept their errors as a matter of course. Jane was sure that she often used CF in her lessons, especially in written exercises. She said that she often collected all her students' errors, and then created some exercises for them purposely, and she might take the advantage of the occasions to give CF. Jane was always worried about hurting students when she was giving CF, particularly, sensitive students and special students. Therefore, she was always trying her best to keep wonderful strategies in mind when she was thinking about giving students CF. For instance, choosing the CF time of not being in a big class or choosing the way of individual correcting. Jane thought that the foci of CF should be on the key grammar points of each unit. She disagreed with giving CF when students were having their oral communication or spoken English show time. She expressed her reason was not to influence students' English fluency and confidence. If the students could express their ideas clearly and the communication became effective, then the errors could surely be neglected.

Beliefs about What Types of CF Should be Focus on

Jane stated that she used four types of CF in her classes: recast, elicitation, metalinguistic feedback, and repetition. She explained that these four types of CF seemed to be recessive, not so straight, which helped the students to accept CF unconsciously. Jane indicated that the other two types of CF, explicit correction and clarification request seemed impolite. She said that she thought her students were equal to her in her mind. She tried her best to be her students' friend.

Overall Impression on CF

Jane was more form-focused when she gave CF in grammar practice. On the other side, she was more meaning-focused when she gave CF in oral English practice. Before the researcher's explanation of CF, she knew very little about it, but she was using it in all her lessons. Jane was very sure that her CF helped her students improve their English learning efficiently. She gave an example from a grammar practice lesson where CF would consolidate students' memory for the short term and the repetition would help students remember the errors' corrected forms in the long term. When talking about how students dealt with Jane's CF, she was not very sure. She said that different students had different attitudes, learning habits and consciousness of CF.

3. Jane's classroom practices on CF

Jane teaches two classes of Grade Three and one class of Grade Four, which consists of 50 students per class. Both the researcher and the second researcher observed Jane for three lessons between May and June, 2014. The classes observed were "Unit 8, Helping Tourists (Part A) " "Unit 8, Helping Tourists (Revision) ", and "Unit 9, Festivals". The classroom observations are summarized below based on two themes that outline Jane's CF practices. Theme One: The types of CF that Jane focused on. Theme Two: The foci of CF in Jane's classroom practices.

In terms of the amount of CF, Jane provided twelve instances of CF during the three lessons. As shown in Table 11, the details of CF types used and the percentages are all very obvious in the table. We can figure out that the only type of CF Jane used in her three classes is recast（100%）.

Table 11　The observation checklist result of Jane's three observed classes

Types of CF	Jane's three classes
Explicit correction	0
Recast	14（100%）
Elicitation	0
Metalinguistic feedback	0
Clarification request	0
Repetition	0

Considering linguistic targets of CF, Table 12 shows that Jane's CF focused mainly on students' grammar errors（50%）, followed by vocabulary errors CF（36%）and pronunciation errors CF（14%）.

Table 12　Number and linguistic targets of Jane's CF in her three observed classes

Grammar	Vocabulary	Pronunciation
7（50%）	5（36%）	2（14%）

Jane used the CF strategy recast when students had grammar errors, vocabulary errors and pronunciation errors. She only used one type of CF "recast", in all her three observed lessons. Jane demonstrated her practices to be meaningful from her statement:

I think recast can spur learners to notice the differences between their own expressions which don't conform to the target language English and the high-level interlocutor's utterances that are much closer to the target language.

（Jane, the fourth interview, July, 2014）

Jane's Classroom Episode 1 (Grammar) (Recast) :

T: Where did you go?

S: I go to ...

T: I went to ...

S: I went to the City Stadium.

(Jane, observation, May, 2014)

In Jane's Classroom Episode 1, she recasts her student's grammar error and her student quickly responds to her feedback by incorporating the right form into the following utterance. It's obvious that incorporation in learners' repair is quite appreciated as it displays that learners have grasped the teacher's recast by being able to apply it.

Jane's Classroom Episode 2 (Vocabulary) (Recast) :

S: I want to go to the City ...

T: City Stadium.

S: I want to go to the City Stadium.

(Jane, observation, May, 2014)

Jane's Classroom Episode 3 (Pronunciation) (Recast) :

S: Here is the bus "s-top".

T: Stop.

S: Bus stop.

(Jane, observation, May, 2014)

Jane's Classroom Episodes 2 and 3, she recasts her students' vocabulary and pronunciation errors. According to the notes of the observation, when Jane recasts her students' errors, she changes her tone, stresses the reformulation and even raises her eyebrows to mark her implicit recast more noticeable for her students. She explained her behavior as below:

As a teacher, I think I should insist the differences of my behavior when I adopt recast to give CF so that my students can receive some regular signals to distinguish from their errors to their correct utterances.

(Jane, the fourth interview, July, 2014)

4. Comparison between Jane's beliefs and practices

The researcher made an analysis of Jane's four interview data and three classroom observations with the help of the second researcher. The researcher examined the observational data to identify how often Jane's CF practices were initiated in her beliefs about CF. This was done to find out to what extent Jane's beliefs were congruent with her practices. To be more clear, the researcher will also show instances where incongruence could be observed.

Jane's beliefs about CF are incongruent with her classroom practices

The inconsistency between Jane's beliefs about CF and her observed practices will be shown in two points:

1. Jane was sure that she often used CF in her lessons. The result of her four classroom observation shows us that Jane only used 14 instances of CF and only one type of the CF in her three lessons, and this tells us that Jane's beliefs are incongruent with her practices in this aspect.

2. Jane stated that she used four types of CF in her classes: recast, elicitation, metalinguistic feedback, and repetition. Actually, she only used one type of CF, which was recast.

Jane's beliefs about CF are congruent with her classroom practices

The consistency between Jane's beliefs about CF and her observed practices will be shown in two points:

1. Jane thought that the foci of CF should be on the key grammar points of each unit. Yes, her practices were congruent with her beliefs on this point according to her three observed lessons.

2. She disagreed to give CF when students were having their oral communication or spoken English show time. She expressed her reason was not to influence students' English fluency and confidence. The researcher noticed the detail that Jane respected her students very much, and she always encouraged her students to talk and accepted every student's active behavior in her class and neglected some errors.

Cross-case Analysis

1. Introduction

The previous part has described the CF practices of the four individual teachers, exploring their pedagogical beliefs about CF. Based on the results reported in the part above, the focus of discussion in this part will be on the commonalities and differences among the four cases in terms of major issues emerging from this study. The researcher will try her best to find out both common patterns and areas of divergence regarding teachers' CF practices, beliefs and influential factors. A cross-analysis is presented in this part.

The first section of this part examines the features of the four teacher participants' CF practices to identify common and diverse characteristics. Two major issues derived from the pertinent data across the four case studies are discussed. These include:

(1) The types of CF that the four teacher participants focused on;

(2) The foci of CF in the four teacher participants' classes.

Next is a comparative account of the four case teachers' pedagogical beliefs about CF. To conclude this cross-case analysis part, salient factors which appear to contribute to CF practices are identified, along with common factors that appear to support or hinder teachers' CF practices. For the sake of facilitating our understanding of each of the case studies, it is necessary to reiterate each participant teacher's educational and professional background. These four participants are all considered to be qualified teachers, as they all have very good reputation among students, students' parents, colleagues, and school leaders. Participants' teaching experience ranged from three to twenty years. All of them received their subject training in teachers' colleges and in-service professional training in their working places and all held a BA or MA degree in English Education. During the time of this study, all four teachers were teaching from Grade Two to Five in Yucai No.3 Primary School.

2. The four participants' practices about CF

Types of CF the four teacher participants focused on

Four major features are derived from the pertinent data across the four case studies. The data can be seen clearly from Table 13.

Feature 1: Different types and amounts of CF used.

According to the results of the four case teachers with a total 12 observed lessons, we can figure out that the total amount of CF used among the four teachers ranges from 12 to 19 in each teacher's three observed classes. The four teachers had different preferences of CF. The two younger teachers used all the six types of CF in their classes. Claire only used three types of CF. And the oldest teacher, Jane, only used one type of CF, recast.

Feature 2: The most frequent type of CF used was recast.

As shown in Table 13, we found that the most common type of teachers' CF in classroom practices in primary school was recast. It was 74% in Ida's three classes, 27% in Vincent's three classes, 75% in Claire's three classes, and 100% in Jane's three classes.

Feature 3: The least frequent type of CF used was clarification request.

Table 13 shows that the least used type of CF in teachers' primary classroom practices was clarification request, which was used by only two of the four teachers and each one used it just once.

Feature 4: The total number of CF occurrences observed among the four primary school teachers was small.

We can see clearly from Table 13 that the amount of the four case teachers'

CF used ranges from 12 to 19, which is not a large amount. The amount of CF also shows us the number of students' learning errors to some extent. The most common explanations from the four teacher participants are: ①The learning content for primary school students is quite simple; ②Each lesson has just a little amount of new knowledge or content; ③Students have good learning habits, showing good preparation or previewing of for the lessons.

Table 13 The observation checklist result of the four teacher participants' three observed classes

Types of CF	Ida's three classes	Vincent's three classes	Claire's three classes	Jane's three classes
Explicit correction	1（5.2%）	3（20%）	0	0
Recast	14（74%）	4（27%）	9（75%）	14（100%）
Elicitation	1（5.2%）	2（13%）	2（17%）	0
Metalinguistic feedback	1（5.2%）	2（13%）	0	0
Clarification request	1（5.2%）	1（7%）	0	0
Repetition	1（5.2%）	3（20%）	1（8%）	0

The foci of CF in the four teacher participants' classes

Feature 1: The most common linguistic target of CF was grammar.

As shown in Table 14, the most common linguistic target of CF was grammar. Participant Ida had a 58% grammar linguistic target of CF in her classroom practices. Vincent had 67%. Claire had 50%. And Jane had 50%. All of their grammar linguistic targets of CF were more than a half of all their whole linguistic targets of CF.

Feature 2: The least noticed linguistic target of CF was pronunciation.

Table 14 shows us that the least noticed linguistic target of CF among the four case teachers was pronunciation. According to the four teachers' explanation, they would like to neglect the learners' errors when they were trying their best to express their ideas or meaning. It's a hard job for primary school students to express their viewpoints in English. So, the students need more encouragement.

Table 14 Number and linguistic targets of the four teacher participants' CF in their three observed classes

Linguistic Targets	Grammar	Vocabulary	Pronunciation
Ida's three classes	11 (58%)	4 (21%)	4 (21%)
Vincent's three classes	10 (67%)	3 (20%)	2 (13%)
Claire's three classes	6 (50%)	4 (33%)	2 (17%)
Jane's three classes	7 (50%)	5 (36%)	2 (14%)

3. The four participants' CF beliefs

Teachers' attitudes towards giving students the correction of errors

The four participants' responses to the second semi-structured interview on their attitudes towards corrective feedback are summarized in Table 15. The columns show the participants' responses to the questions. The first row of Table 15 provides the four teacher participants' opinions on students' making errors in language acquisition. 100% of the teacher participants indicate that errors in students' English learning are unavoidable. The three participants support the main idea of the second question which is about teachers correcting students' errors immediately, while only one of them is not sure. From a practical viewpoint, correcting errors immediately is impossible for English teachers in Shenzhen now. Because most of the English teachers in Shenzhen teach three classes and each class has about 50 students. Although it seems impossible, the idea of immediate correction is preferable.

Essentially, the three participants agree with the idea of the effectiveness of correction. Only one of them has an uncertain response. All the participants agree with the fourth question, which is that students feel it's hard to notice their own errors. These two findings clearly demonstrate teachers' positive perception of correction of students' errors.

The fifth and sixth questions are both about correcting students' every error in speaking and writing. The attitudes towards correcting students' every speaking error are quite straightforward. All the participants disagree with the idea that teachers should correct all students' speaking errors. On contrast, most of them（75%）agree with the idea that teachers should correct all students' writing errors, and only one participant（25%）is not sure. Teachers are aware of students' writing difficulties, so feedback seems extremely important and necessary. Teachers know that students keep making the same common errors as teachers have repeatedly pointed out to them.

The seventh question is that correction of oral errors in class undermines the learner's self-esteem. Teacher participants' responses are diversified. One of them is negative, two of them are positive, and one of them is uncertain. This finding shows that teachers seem to worry about undermining their students' self-esteem. Kavaliauskiene and Anusiene's survey about students' attitudes towards correction of errors（Kavaliauskiene & Anusiene, 2012）shows that students do not worry about their self-esteem being undermined. It is possible, therefore, that these students' responses can be good news for teachers, and that error correction is not expected to affect their motivation or willingness to perfect English learning skills.

The eighth question is that individual correction of errors in writing is useful. All the participants（100%）agree with it, which shows that teachers think it's useful to have individual error correction in writing as it facilitates personal learning. To develop students' English language awareness, teachers feel that a personalized learning of English and getting relevant feedback to the individual student's performance are very important. 75% of the teacher participants find students' peer feedback beneficial. Only one participant（25%）feels unsure. The possible cause of this perception is that peers can encourage and help each other, and they can understand each other easily.

Table 15 The result of the second semi-structured interview about teachers' attitudes towards giving students the correction of errors

Main ideas of the interview questions	Strongly disagree or disagree	Not sure	Agree or strongly agree
1. Errors are natural.			Jane, Claire, Ida, Vincent
2. Immediate correction is good for students' learning.		Claire	Jane, Ida, Vincent
3. Teacher correction is generally effective.		Claire	Jane, Ida, Vincent
4. It's hard for students to notice their own errors.			Jane, Claire, Ida, Vincent
5. All errors in speaking must be corrected.	Jane, Claire, Ida, Vincent		
6. All errors in writing must be corrected.		Claire	Jane, Ida, Vincent
7. Correction of oral errors in class undermines the learner's self-esteem.	Jane	Ida	Claire, Vincent
8. Individual correction of errors in writing is useful.			Jane, Claire, Ida, Vincent
9. Peer feedback is beneficial.		Ida	Jane, Claire, Vincent

Teachers' foci of CF

During the interviews, all four participants were asked to talk about their understanding about the usage of CF and their foci of CF. All four teachers emphasized the importance of CF in daily English class. They all had the same similar concept that CF helped students to have correct English expression habits and avoid the development of error fossilization. According to Ida, her foci of CF were students' pronunciation errors and frequently existing errors. Compared with Ida, Vincent,

Claire and Jane paid more attention to each unit's main knowledge points. Vincent pointed out the emphasis and difficulties of each learning unit of the textbook. Claire's foci of CF were on the important sentence patterns of each unit. Jane indicated that her foci of CF were each unit's main grammar points.

In summary of the foci of CF, the four teachers' CF beliefs were largely congruent with their practices. There were only a few inconsistencies between what they said and believed and their classroom behaviors. In their practices, their common foci of CF were mainly on grammar. According to Ida's three class observations, she focused on grammar largely（58%）, and then pronunciation（21%）.

Teachers' beliefs about what types of CF should be focus on

In the interviews, all of the four teachers expressed their preferences about what types of CF they would focus on. Ida preferred to use these three types of CF: recast, elicitation and repetition for the sake of protecting students, making the students understand easily, and quickly noticing their errors. Vincent stated that he used two types of CF in his classes: elicitation and clarification request. Claire stated that she used all the six types of CF in her classes: explicit correction, recast, elicitation, metalinguistic feedback, clarification request and repetition. Jane stated that she used four types of CF in her classes: recast, elicitation, metalinguistic feedback and repetition.

In summary of the CF types, the four participants' beliefs were incongruent with their practices. Based on the classroom observation notes, we found that Ida and Vincent used all the six types of CF in their classes. Claire used three types of the CF in her actual classes. Jane only used one type of CF—recast.

Teachers' overall impression of CF

There were several cases where the four teacher participants' beliefs differed among themselves, and there were some aspects where there were no differences, and this was reflected in the teachers' stated beliefs. According to the analysis of the interview data, we can sum up the teachers' overall impression of CF in several viewpoints.

Viewpoint 1: Before the training of CF, all of the four participants did not know the technical term CF, but they all indicated that they had been using it in all their lessons.

Viewpoint 2: The four teachers all agreed that teachers' CF helped students improve their English learning efficiently.

Viewpoint 3: They all emphasized the importance of repeating the same CF frequently in order to help the students consolidate the correct form of English words, phases, pronunciation, grammar, and so on.

Viewpoint 4: They all worried about undermining their students' self-esteem when giving them CF. Therefore, they confirmed that they would try their best to encourage the learners, especially when the learners were expressing their ideas in oral communication activities.

Viewpoint 5: Ida and Claire had the same confidence about their beliefs matching their teaching practices. But Vincent and Jane indicated that only sometimes their beliefs and teaching practices were matched.

4. Factors affecting teachers' CF practices

After finishing the previous two parts, which were the four teachers' practices about CF and their CF beliefs, the researcher sprouted another question, asking what factors impacted these four teacher participants' CF practices. To answer this question, the researcher analyzed all the data, including the interview data and classroom observation data. Furthermore, the researcher and the second researcher compared all the data. The findings are presented below, which are classified into three main categories: beliefs, educational experiences, and training and teaching experiences.

Category One: Beliefs

The teachers' beliefs about what types of CF should be focus on, as well as their beliefs of the foci of CF, appear to heavily influence their actual CF practices. Ida indicated that she would put the foci of CF on pronunciation, because she believed this was a very important aspect of communication and the primary English learning for students. As the classroom observation data were revealed, although Ida's most common foci of CF were on grammar（58%）, Ida's correction of pronunciation（21%）was much more than the other three teachers.

Category Two：Educational experiences

All of the four teachers discussed how their educational experiences, especially as language learners, have been influencing their CF practices. Jane recalled one of her former English teachers with an idolizing mood. She introduced her idolized teacher's wonderful English pronunciation, teaching methods or strategies, respect for students, and so on.

Category Three：Training and teaching experiences

As expected, all the four teachers credited their recent CF explanation which they called a training from the researcher, and this is one of the factors that informed their CF practices. Ida and Claire mentioned that they were impacted by their experienced colleagues in terms of their English teaching, including their CF practices.

5. Summary

The foci in this chapter are mainly on the results of this study among the case studies, the commonalities and differences of the four cases, and influential factors affecting teachers' CF practices.

In the next chapter, the researcher will address the research questions which are the foci of the study. Therefore, the major theoretical contribution of the study will be presented, followed by implications for CF practices, the study's limitations and suggestions for further research.

CHAPTER 5

5

CONCLUSION AND IMPLICATIONS

Introduction

This chapter presents the final conclusions regarding findings described and analyzed in the previous chapters. Based on the findings, several major implications are posed.

To begin this chapter, the researcher will first address the three research questions which are the core purposes of this study. Teachers' CF beliefs, teachers' CF practices and beliefs compatible or incompatible will be summarized. Implications for CF practices will then be presented, followed by recommendations for CF further research.

Summary of Findings

The main purpose of this study is to provide a picture of what beliefs primary school teachers hold about CF and their CF practices. The researcher carried out four case studies of English teachers in a primary school in the city of Shenzhen. Data collection methods chosen for this study were comprised of four interviews and L2 classroom observations.

Data focused on four case teachers in one school in China. However, the researcher has confidence that it also speaks to a lot of researchers and educators. The findings revolve around the three major research questions of this study, as listed below.

1. What beliefs do EFL teachers hold about corrective feedback?

2. How do EFL teachers practice CF in actual primary English classrooms?

3. To what extent are EFL teachers' beliefs about corrective feedback congruent with their observed teaching practices?

1. What beliefs do EFL teachers hold about CF?

The first research question deals with EFL primary school teachers' views on CF. Their perceived CF features were a major research area. Data regarding teachers' CF beliefs in this study were obtained from four different steps of interviews, which were all semi-structured interviews. According to this study's findings, teachers' CF beliefs are summarized in point format below.

(1) All teacher participants believed that CF was important for EFL

classrooms.

(2) All teachers believed that CF was very helpful for EFL students' English learning.

(3) All teachers disagreed that all errors in speaking must be corrected.

(4) All teachers agreed that errors were natural.

(5) All teachers thought that it was hard for students to notice their own errors.

(6) All teachers were very sure that individual correction of errors in writing was useful.

(7) The four teachers except the youngest teacher Ida, thought that peer feedback was beneficial.

(8) The teachers all emphasized the importance of repeating the same CF frequently in order to help the students consolidate the correct form of English learning.

(9) The teachers all worried about undermining their students' self-esteem when giving them CF.

(10) Before the researcher's explanation of CF, all of four participants did not know the technical term CF, but they all indicated that they had been using it in all their lessons.

(11) All teachers believed that giving CF to one individual student could influence the whole class.

(12) All teachers advocated activating and encouraging students to participate in CF activities. They all valued students' participation.

(13) All teachers indicated that they would pay more attention to students' expressing meaning and neglect their errors when students were having oral communication.

(14) The teachers all believed that efficient in-service training could help improve their CF practices.

(15) They all believed that they learned a lot from more experienced teachers on their CF practices and all their teaching practices.

（16）Ida's foci of CF were students' pronunciation errors and frequently existing errors. Compared with Ida, Vincent, Claire and Jane paid more attention on each unit's main knowledge points.

（17）All teachers except Vincent were sure that they often used CF in their lessons. Vincent thought that the rate of his CF use was not very frequent.

（18）All teachers expressed that they would accept better CF methods or strategies if they had the chance to know some.

Summary：Four teacher participants have their own understanding and beliefs about CF. They treat CF as a very helpful and important teaching strategy for students' EFL learning. All of the four case teachers agree that errors are natural existing during EFL learners' learning. Nevertheless, they prefer to give CF to students' written errors and some of the spoken errors instead of all the spoken errors. Their common reasons are that comprehension comes first when students are trying their best to express their ideas in English, and teachers should try not to undermine students' self-esteem when giving CF. Students' active participation is valued greatly. Three of the four case teachers view peer correction as better than teachers' CF, but teachers' CF is necessary and meaningful in the EFL teaching. Teachers emphasized repeating the same error correction when giving CF. The foci of CF should be like the difficult knowledge points and students frequently existing errors. For the purpose of improving teachers' giving CF strategy level, all of the four teacher participants would like to take related efficient in-service training.

2. How do EFL teachers practice CF in actual primary English classrooms?

The second research question deals with EFL primary school teachers' CF practices. Their real-life CF teaching practices were a major research area. In this study, data regarding teachers' CF practices were obtained from each case teacher's three classroom observations and total 12 observations. According to the findings, the features of teachers' CF real-life practices are also summarized in point format below.

（1）All the teacher participants were dedicated to the teaching job and they designed and organized CF teaching activities with great enthusiasm. Jane did best in this aspect. She collected all students' errors and recalled the errors her former students had and prepared the coming lesson's CF activities carefully with great passion.

(2) All teachers adapted the six types of CF's classification after the researcher's CF explanation and would think about it when they were planning their lessons.

(3) Some teachers (Vincent and Claire, in particular) specifically preferred to provide opportunities and encouragement for students to be engaged in CF giving tasks, and their students behaved more actively in correcting other students' errors.

(4) All teachers encouraged students to participate in class activities actively, especially in CF activities.

(5) The total amount of CF used among the four teachers ranged from 12 to 19 in each teacher's three classes, which meant that the amount of CF in primary school teachers' EFL classes was similar.

(6) The four teachers had different preferences of CF types. The two younger teachers used all six types of CF in their classes. Claire used three types of CF, and the oldest teacher Jane used only one type of CF, "recast".

(7) The most common type of teachers' CF in EFL classroom practices in primary school was recast.

(8) The least frequently used type of CF in EFL classroom practices in primary school was clarification request.

(9) The most common linguistic target of CF in EFL classroom practices in primary school was grammar.

(10) The low graders' EFL teacher Ida paid more attention to pronunciation than the high grader teachers.

(11) The least noticed linguistic target of CF among the four case teachers' classroom practices was pronunciation.

(12) All of the four teachers refrained from giving CF when students were

having their oral communication or spoken English show time.

(13) All of the four teachers did not correct all students' speaking errors, especially in Claire's and Vincent's classes.

Summary: The four teacher participants were dedicated to the teaching job and they designed and organized CF teaching activities with great enthusiasm. As the oldest teacher among the four cases, Jane did best in this aspect. She collected all students' errors and recalled the errors her former students had and prepared the coming lesson's CF activities carefully with great passion. Vincent and Claire, in particular, provided opportunities and encouragement for students to be engaged in CF giving tasks, and their students behaved more actively in correcting other students' errors. The total amount of CF used among the four teachers was very close, which ranged from 12 to 19 in each teacher's three classes. The four case teachers had different preferences of CF types, and the most common type of CF in the 12 observed classes was recast. The most common linguistic target of CF was grammar. All of the four teacher participants refrained from giving CF when students were having their oral communication or spoken English show time, just like they stated in the interviews that comprehension came first at that moment.

3. To what extent are EFL teachers' beliefs about CF congruent with their observed teaching practices?

The third research question aims to ascertain to what extent EFL teachers' beliefs about CF were incongruent or congruent with their real-life CF teaching practices. To answer this question, classroom observations were made and teachers' behaviors and the beliefs teachers stated were examined. According to the findings of this study, the chief features of teachers' beliefs about CF are incongruent or congruent with their CF teaching practices as summarized in the list which follows.

Teachers' beliefs about CF incongruent with their practices

Feature 1: Most teachers believed that they used CF frequently in class. In fact, the amount of CF used in actual practices was small. All of the four case teachers stated that they often used CF in their classes in the interview. According to the classroom observations, we know that the amount of the four case teachers' used CF ranges from 12 to 19, which is not a large amount.

Feature 2: All teachers stated that it was unnecessary to have CF when students were having oral communication. Sometimes, some teachers could not help to stop students' talking and give CF in the oral communicating time. For example, the case teacher Vincent stopped his students' English oral expressing and gave CF in the classroom observations.

Feature 3: Teachers all emphasized the importance of repeating the same CF frequently in order to help the students consolidate the correct form of English learning, but it's hard to find their repeating behavior of the same error correction.

Teachers' beliefs about CF congruent with their practices

Feature 1: Teachers all thought CF was important and helpful for EFL students' English learning. They designed and organized CF teaching activities with great enthusiasm in their EFL classroom practices.

Feature 2: Most teachers considered peer feedback to be beneficial. In practice, they preferred to provide opportunities and encouragement for students to be engaged in CF giving tasks, and the students were actually quite active in correcting other students' errors.

Feature 3: Teachers all chose the CF type recast as their preference. The result of classroom practice observations showed that the most common type of teachers' CF was recast. All of the four case teachers used recast most frequently.

Feature 4: Only a small part of the teachers stated that they liked the CF type clarification request. The real-life practice observation result showed the least frequently type of CF used was clarification request.

Feature 5: Teachers indicated that the present common English teaching approach in China was still the examination-oriented assessment system. They said that they had to pay more attention to students' grammar learning, key sentence understanding and main knowledge points mastering in the in-depth interviews. The fact of the practices proved that the most common linguistic target of CF in EFL primary school classroom practice was grammar.

Feature 6: Most teachers stated that they would pay more attention to pronunciation in the low graders and more attention to grammar in the high graders. In fact, the low graders' EFL teacher Ida paid more attention to pronunciation than the high grader teachers.

Feature 7: Teachers all said in the interview that they worried about undermining their students' self-esteem when giving them CF. Moreover, all teachers disagreed that all errors in speaking must be corrected. The real-life practices proved that teachers refrained from giving CF when students were having their oral communication or spoken English show time, and they did not correct all students' speaking errors in class.

As discussed in the cross-case analysis and in the main findings of this study, the four case teachers' beliefs about CF were largely congruent with their CF teaching practices. Thompson argued in 1992 that the relationship between practices and beliefs was a two-way street. Not only do beliefs influence practice, but also beliefs can be shaped by practice. A trend emerged from the results of this study here: the more theoretical knowledge about teaching the teachers had, the better they implemented CF in practice and the students learned more effectively.

Implications

From the findings of this study, notable implications can be found for English teaching in China.

Firstly, it is necessary for teachers to have professional pre-service and in-service training, especially, training with specific topics and contents step-by-step. According to the investigation of the research, most teachers were lacking of professional training that resulted in their insufficiency in English teaching. For example, before the researcher's CF explanation of this study, all the case teachers did not know the technical term CF, which meant that teachers were teaching just according to their sensation or experience instead of basing it on scientifical pedagogical theory. More training courses are needed so that teachers can understand and know better how to implement the teaching objectives using scientific teaching methods. Teachers need to build their confidence with strong pedagogical theory and should be encouraged to experiment with new teaching approaches, to learn from each other and always make progress.

Secondly, serious English examination reform efforts in China are imperative. The examination-oriented assessment system is a big obstacle for EFL teachers to implement the communicative teaching approach, which can really help students to learn useful English and apply English with vigour. China's present situation tells us that the government has started to have reforms on English examination recently, which brings English teachers great news.

Thirdly, English teachers and education policy-makers are encouraged and supported to have empirical research of English classrooms. Although CF is a very famous technical term in the theory of teaching methodology, there is very little discussion of how CF is actually implemented in school settings. There is a lack of empirical research of CF giving in China's EFL teaching practices. The empirical research conducted in EFL classroom settings may provide the most reliable evidence for education policy-making. Moreover, it may be very helpful and practical for EFL teachers to spend time in observing the best criterion for their actual practices.

Limitations of the Study and Suggestions for Further Research

Although the researcher has tried her best in this study, this research inevitably has its shortcomings that deserve our attention. Some limitations of the study and suggestions for further research can be identified.

Firstly, the study involved just one school and only four case teachers. The sample was small, which affected the validity of the study to some degree. Thus, a broader and larger sample is suggested to be involved in the future studies.

Secondly, classroom observation was focused on only four teachers' three classes. The collected data were not at full-scale. So a long term research was suggested for future research.

Thirdly, even though with 13 years of teaching experience, it's the author's first time to have such a research. The data collection is incomplete to some extent from lack of experience. Some variables such as types of lessons have not been considered. So it is necessary to take more variables into consideration for further research.

APPENDIXES

Beliefs Inventory from Johnson

Name: Years of Teaching English Grades of Your Present Teaching Students

Instructions: Please read all 15 statements, and then select five statements that most closely reflect your beliefs about how English as a second language is learned and how English as a second language should be taught.

(Rule-based)	1.Language can be thought of as a set of grammatical structures which are learned consciously and controlled by the language learner.
(Function-based)	2. As long as EFL students understand what they are saying, they are actually learning the language.
(Rule-based)	3. When EFL students make oral errors, it helps to correct them and later teach a short lesson explaining why they made that error.
(Skill-based)	4. As long as EFL students listen to, practice, and remember the language which native speakers use, they are actually learning the language.
(Rule-based)	5. EFL students generally need to understand the grammatical rules of English in order to become fluent in the language.

(Skill-based) 6. When EFL students make oral errors, it usually helps to provide them with lots of oral practices with the language patterns which seem to cause them difficulty.

(Function-based) 7. Language can be thought of as meaningful communication and is learned subconsciously in non-academic, social situations.

(Rule-based) 8. If EFL students understand some of the basic grammatical rules of the language, they can usually make lots of new sentences on their own.

(Function-based) 9. Usually it is more important for EFL students to focus on what they are trying to say than how to say it.

(Skill-based) 10. If EFL students practice the language patterns of native speakers, they can make new sentences based on those language patterns which they have already practiced.

(Rule-based) 11. It's important to provide clear, frequent, precise presentations of grammatical structures during English language instruction.

(Skill-based) 12. Language can be described as a set of behaviors which are mastered through lots of drill and practice with the language patterns of native speakers.

(Function-based) 13. When EFL students make oral errors, it is best to ignore them, as long as you can understand what they are trying to say.

(Skill-based) 14. EFL students usually need to master some of the basic listening and speaking skills before they can begin to read and write.

(Function-based)	15. It's not necessary to actually teach EFL students how to speak English. They usually begin speaking English on their own.

Lesson Plan Analysis Task

您好！非常感谢您能在百忙中抽出时间完成这么一份关于教学信念的调查。您的英文名（English name）：________。您的教龄（years of teaching）：________。请您完成以下两个小任务：

Task 1, please describe an ideal EFL classroom in your eyes.（请您描述您理想中的英语课堂, 如学生的表现、教师的表现、课堂学习氛围等）（此题用中英文回答都可以）

____

____

____

Task 2, there are three lesson plans designed for teaching the same grammatical concept（modals：can, will, may, and might）for you to have a look. Please choose one that is similar to what you often teach in your class.（请选择一篇跟您平时给学生上课形式相似的教案）

I choose Lesson Plan ________.

Lesson Plan 1（Skill-based）

The teacher has decided on the following procedures to teach the meaning and the use of the modals can, will, may, and might.

Dialogue

Sue：Are you going to the beach tomorrow?

Lisa：I am not sure. It may rain. I might go to the movies.

Sue：Can I come along? I love movies!

Lisa：Sure!

Sue：Will you call me if you decide to go to the movies?

Lisa：Sure, can I have your number?

Sue：663-6354

Lisa：OK, I will call you in the morning.

Sue：Great! We can go to the the theater by bus.

Lisa：OK, I will talk to you tomorrow.

Sue：Bye!

a. Repeat the dialogue. Ask students to repeat the dialogue in turn.

b. Ask students to identify the sentences which contain modals.

c. Write the sentences from the dialogue which contain modals on the board.

Exercise 1：Ask and answer each question.

1. Is Lisa going to the beach tomorrow?
2. Is the weather going to be nice tomorrow?
3. Can they go to the theater by bus?
4. Will Lisa call Sue in the morning or the afternoon?
5. Will it be sunny or rainy tomorrow?

Exercise 2：Use the cue word to make a new sentence.

1. It may rain tomorrow.（be sunny）（snow）（be cold）（be windy）

2. We can go to the theater by bus.（by taxi）（the museum）（the stadium）（by car）

3. I might go to the movies.（beach）（game）（store）

4. She can swim.（might / tomorrow）（will / on Sunday）

5. We can get to the airport by train.（might / faster by taxi）（will / faster by helicopter）

6. I can finish my homework in two hours.（might / in one hour）（will / before I go to bed）

Exercise 3：Read each situation aloud. Ask students to think of actions which might solve each problem.

Encourage them to use can, will, may, or might in their oral responses.

1. Some students are walking in the forest. It is almost dark, and they are lost.

2. You are visiting New York City for the first time. You are lost and you don't have a map.

3. You took a taxi from the airport to your hotel. When you tried to pay the driver you had no money.

4. You just finished a meal at a nice restaurant and you realized you forgot your wallet.

Lesson Plan 2（Rule-based）

The teacher has decided on the following procedures to teach the meaning and the use of the modals can, will, may, and might.

Modal Auxiliaries： Introduction

Auxiliary + The Simple Form of a Verb

Can：I can speak English.

Will：I will be in class tomorrow.（form of a verb）

Will：Will you call me tomorrow?

May：It may rain tomorrow.

Might：It might rain tomorrow.

CORRECT：I can speak English.

INCORRECT：I can to speak English.

Explain and discuss

"Can" expresses ability or possibility in the present or future.

"Will" expresses ability in the future tense.

"Will you" is used as a polite way to ask a question. It can also mean asking for someone's help.

"May" and "might" express possibility in the present or future and they have the same meaning.

Exercise 1：Ask and Answer. Use can.

a. What abilities and talents do you have? Tell the class about some of the things you can do.

Can you swim? Can you play the piano?

b. Ask a classmate if he or she has a certain ability or talent.

1. Tom wants to go to the zoo. Tell him what he can see at the zoo.
2. John wants a hammer. Tell him where he can get a hammer.
3. Sandra has to go to the airport tomorrow. How can she get there?
4. Jeff is bored on the weekend. Tell him some things he can do on the weekend.
5. Jenny wants to eat out tonight. Where can she get a good meal?

Exercise 2：Answer each of the following questions using may and might.

T：What are you going to do tomorrow?

S：I don't know. I may go downtown. Or I might go skiing.

1. What are you going to do tomorrow night?
2. What's the weather going to be like tomorrow?
3. What does Sue have in her purse?
4. What are you going to do after class?
5. What are you going to do during vacation?

Exercise 3：Have students read each situation.

Ask students to write five sentences which contain the modals can, will, may, or might to solve each problem. Ask students to read their sentences to the class.

1. Some students are walking in the forest. It is almost dark, and they are lost.

2. You are visiting New York City for the first time. You are lost and you don't have a map.

3. You took a taxi from the airport to your hotel. When you tried to pay the driver you had no money.

4. You just finished a meal at a nice restaurant and you realized you forgot your wallet.

Lesson Plan 3 (Function-based)

The teacher has decided on the following procedures to teach the meaning and the use of the modals can, will, may, and might.

Congratulations! You have just won a "Dream Vacation". Choose one of the following trips as your prize and check (√) your choice.

( ) A four-month luxury cruise around the world.

( ) A one-month safari in the Australian outback.

( ) A three-week mountain-climbing vacation in the Himalayas.

( ) A two-month drive from Norway to Spain.

Exercise 1: Get into a group with people who choose the same trip as you.

Talk about your trip: Where will you go? What will you bring along? What can you do there? What problems might you have once you get there? What can you do to prepare for the trip?

Make a list of ten things you will take with you.

Make a list of five things you can do to prepare for the trip.

Make a list of eight things you will do when you get there.

Make a list of five possible problems you might have on this trip.

Exercise 2: Take turns.

Tell the class where you're going, what you will bring with you, and one of the problems you might have.

Your classmates will suggest solutions.

Exercise 3: Write a letter to a friend telling him / her about your "Dream Vacation".

Describe all the things you will take and what you will do when you get there. Also mention some of the problems you might have and ask for suggestions. Read your letter to a classmate before sending it off in the mail!

Observation Checklist of Teachers' Corrective Feedback

Table 1 Observation checklist of open class

CF / Participants	When	What	How	Form-focused / Meaning-focused
Ida				
Vincent				
Jane				
Claire				

Notes: "When" includes: ①interaction between the teacher and the individual student or students (TS); pair work (PW); group work (GW); ②errors of grammar, genre, and content.

"What" includes students' errors.

"How" includes teachers' CF.

Table 2　Sorting table of six types of teachers' CF after observation of open class

Types of CF Participants	Ida	Vincent	Jane	Claire
Explicit correction				
Recast				
Elicitation				
Metalinguistic feedback				
Clarification request				
Repetition				

Notes：The common classes have the same observation checklist and the sorting table.

The First Interview Questions about Teachers' Beliefs about Teaching English

1. Please tell me something about your own experience of language learning. Do you think your own language learning experience influences the way you teach?

2. What are the sources of your belief in your teaching?

3. Do you give your lessons as you planned or based on the actual situation?

4. What teaching activities do you often design, student-centered or teacher-centered?

5. Do you pay more attention to accuracy or fluency of students' spoken English and written English, accuracy or fluency?

6. Do you think your teaching beliefs match your teaching practices? If not, what is the problem?

The Second Interview Questions about Teachers' Attitude towards the Correction of Students' Errors

Teachers' Attitude towards the Correction of Students' Errors

1. Are errors natural? Why?

2. Is immediate correction good for students' learning? Why?

3. Is teachers' correction generally effective? Why?

4. Is it hard for students to notice their own errors? Why?

5. Should all errors in speaking be corrected? Why?

6. Should all errors in writing be corrected? Why?

7. Does correction of oral errors in class undermine the learner's self-esteem? Why?

8. Is individual correction of errors in writing useful? Why?

9. Is peer feedback beneficial? Why?

The Third Interview Questions about Teachers' Beliefs about CF in Daily Teaching

1. When you give corrective feedback to students, are you more form-focused or meaning-focused?

2. Before the training of corrective feedback, what do you know about corrective feedback?

3. What corrective feedback of the six types do you prefer to use in your classroom and in correcting students' writing?

4. What's your linguistic foci of corrective feedback, grammar, pronunciation or vocabulary?

5. Do you think teachers' corrective feedback can help students improve their English learning effectively? If yes, how?

6. How do you think your students deal with the corrective feedback given by you?

The Fourth Interview Questions

1. 你认为Corrective Feedback（CF）重要吗？

2. 你在课堂上用得多吗？

3. 什么情况下必须用CF？什么时候你觉得没必要用？

4. 给学生CF时，你是否会有所顾虑？比如顾虑学生的面子。

5. 用CF时你为什么喜欢用这几种？不用其他的原因是什么？

6. 学生在你的课堂上开口发言表达的机会多吗？参与发言的面广吗？

7. 你喜欢用哪几种CF？但观察了你的三节课，却是这样的情况：……你认为是什么原因导致了不一致？

Observation Checklist of Teachers' CF

Table 1　Observation Checklist of Teachers' Corrective Feedback 1

Participant：Ida

Student：Class One, Grade Two

Topic：Unit 9, My clothes — Open Class

Time：May 14, 2014, Wednesday

The first observation notes

CF Participants	Who	What	How
Ida	Teacher and one individual student	1. S：I'm wearing blue T-shirt. T：I'm wearing a blue T-shirt.	Recast
	Teacher and the whole class	2. Pronunciation error：blouse Ss：Blouse[brəʊz]. T：Please say after me "blouse" ['blaʊz].	
		3. Ss：Shoes [ʃɔːz]. T：Shoes ['ʃuːz].	
	Teacher and one individual student	4. S：Summer is cold and nice. T：Summer is cold and nice?	Repetition
		5. S：I need a new shoes. T：I need a pair of new shoes. Follow me...	Recast
	Teacher and one individual student	6. S：I need a n... T-shirt. T：New. S：I need a new T-shirt.	Recast

续 表

CF / Participants	Who	What	How
Ida	Group work	7. S1：What else do you need? S2：I have a new T-shirt. T：Need. S2：I need a new T-shirt.	Recast

Table 2 Observation Checklist of Teachers' Corrective Feedback 2

Participant：Ida

Student：Class One, Grade Two

Topic：Unit 10, Activities — Open Class

Time：May 21, 2014, Wednesday

The second observation notes

CF / Participants	Who	What	How
Ida	Teacher and one individual student	1. S：I can riding a bicycle. T：I can ride a bicycle. T：can+ 动词原形 T：like + doing	Recast Metalinguistic feedback
	Teacher and one individual student：Drive a train one by one	2. S1：I can sleeping. T：I like sleeping.	Recast
		3. S2：I can running. T：I can run.	
		4. S3：I can swimming. T：I can swim.	
		5. S4：I can dancing. T：I can dance.	

Table 3 Observation Checklist of Teachers' Corrective Feedback 3

Participant: Ida

Student: Class Three, Grade Two

Topic: Unit 12, A girl and three bears

Time: June 6, 2014, Friday

The third observation notes

CF Participants	Who	What	How
Ida	Teacher and one individual student	1. S: Lucy has small eyes and mouth. T: Only one mouth. Two eyes we say eyes. So, we say a mouth. S: Lucy has small eyes and a mouth.	Elicitation
		2. S: She has long hair. T: Not long hair, short. S: She has short hair.	(Pay attention to meaning) Explicit correction
		3. S: Lucy is tired. (pronunciation) T: Lucy is tired.	Recast
		4. S: Lucy is baby. T: Lucy is a baby.	
		5. T: If it is rainy, what would you do? S: I would be in home and play computer games. T: I would be at home and play computer games.	
		6. S: I will go swim. T: I will go swimming or I will go to swim.	
		7. S: It's sunny. Let's go to Paris. T: Pardon? S: Paris. (pronunciation) T: Paris.	Clarification request

续 表

CF / Participants	Who	What	How
Ida	Teacher and one individual student	8. S：I'm hungry, thirsty and tired. （thirsty — pronunciation） T：Follow me, thirsty.	Recast
		9. S：I am hungry. I want some hamburgers. （pronunciation） T：Hamburgers.	

Table 4　Observation Checklist of Teachers' Corrective Feedback 4

Participant：Vincent

Student：Class Four, Grade Five

Topic：Unit 6, Typhoon（Exercises）

Time：May 26, 2014, Monday

The first observation notes

CF / Participants	Who	What	How
Vincent	Teacher and the whole class	1. Ss：Asia.（pronunciation） T：Asia. T：Read after me "Asia".	Recast
	Teacher and one individual student	2. S1：Putted. T：No, put—put, read—read, cut—cut, hit—hit.	Explicit correction Metalinguistic feedback
		3. S2：I don't go out. T：Yesterday. S2：... T：I didn't go out, do—did, don't—didn't.	Metalinguistic feedback

Table 5 Observation Checklist of Teachers' Corrective Feedback 5

Participant: Vincent

Student: Class Four, Grade Four

Topic: Sports Day — Open Class

Time: June 15, 2014, Sunday

The second observation notes

<table>
<tr><th>CF
Participants</th><th>Who</th><th>What</th><th>How</th></tr>
<tr><td rowspan="5">Vincent</td><td rowspan="3">Teacher and one individual student</td><td>1. S1: He can swimming.
T: He can do swimming.
He can swim.</td><td>Recast</td></tr>
<tr><td>2. S2: I can playing table tennis.
T: I can playing?
S2: I can play table tennis.</td><td>Repetition</td></tr>
<tr><td>3. S3: I can play football.
I can high jump.
T: I can high jump?
S3: I can play the high jump.
T: No, do.
S3: I can do the high jump.</td><td>Repetition
Explicit correction</td></tr>
<tr><td>Teacher and the whole class</td><td>4. S4: I can make a ball.
T: Who can make a ball?
Ss: Laughing...
T: You can catch a ball.</td><td rowspan="2">Recast</td></tr>
<tr><td>Teacher and one individual student</td><td>5. S5: I can't ball.
T: Throw a ball.
S5: I can't throw a ball.</td></tr>
</table>

续 表

CF Participants	Who	What	How
Vincent	Teacher and the whole class	6. S6：I can play foot-ball.（pronunciation） T：Foot-ball? Ss：Laughing... T：Say after me：football, basketball, table tennis.	Repetition
		7. S7：I can long jump, but I can't high jump. T： Are they right? Ss： No, can do and can't do. T： Yes, but the others are right. （Vincent擅长引导全体同学一起来帮忙纠错。）	Elicitation
	Teacher and one individual student	8. S8：I can swimming, but I can't high jump. T：Some errors. I can do, not I can swimming. I can't do. I can't do the high jump.	
	Group work	9. S9：What is Bob going to do? S10：Bob is going to running. S11：What's Tim going to do? S12：He is do the high jump. T：Errors: He is going to run, not running. "Be going to do". He is going to do the high jump.	Explicit correction

Table 6 Observation Checklist of Teachers' Corrective Feedback 6

Participant: Vincent

Student: Class Three, Grade Five

Topic: Stories enjoying — Open Class

Time: June 20, 2014, Friday

The third observation notes

CF / Participants	Who	What	How
Vincent	Teacher and one individual student	1. S1: Did Anna father cook the rabbit for dinner? T: Did Anna's father cook the rabbit for dinner?	Recast
		2. S2: Miss Li gives her a bike / baɪ /. (pronunciation) T: Pardon? S2: Bike / baɪ / . T: Bike.	Clarification request
		3. S3: Miss Li give Anna a bike. Is Anna happy?	give—gives没有纠错, 只关注了关键句 "Is Anna happy?"
		4. S4: Who is they new friend?	they—their没有纠错, 只关注了关键词语 new friend
		5. S5: When time for dinner? T: Any errors? S6: What's the time for dinner? T: Any other answers?	Elicitation

续 表

CF Participants	Who	What	How
Vincent	Teacher and one individual student	S7：When's Anna's dinner? T：What time... When... (Vincent 擅长归类对比，讲解语法点，如： how many 与 how much 的区别。 what time与when 的区别。 也许是期末将至，Vincent在上课时侧重语法讲解。)	Elicitation

Table 7　Observation Checklist of Teachers' Corrective Feedback 7

Participant：Claire

Student：Class Two, Grade Five

Topic：Unit 7, Summer holidays（Part C）

Time：May 29, 2014, Thursday

The first observation notes

CF Participants	Who	What	How
Claire	Teacher and one individual student	1. S1：I read / ri: d / a book last night. T：Read / ri: d / ? S1：I read / red / a book last night.	Repetition
		2. S2：I break it yesterday. T：Broke. S2：I broke it yesterday.	Recast

续 表

CF Participants	Who	What	How
Claire	Group work（四人小组表演时Claire纠错比较少。）	3.S3：I were to the restaurant.（pronunciation） Ss：Went. T：I went to the restaurant. It's the pronunciation error. Were and went are different. S3： I went to the restaurant.	Recast Elicitation

Table 8　Observation Checklist of Teachers' Corrective Feedback 8

Participant：Claire

Student：Class Five, Grade Two

Topic：Unit 2, I'm Danny（Period 2）— Open Class

Time：June 12, 2014, Thursday

The second observation notes

CF Participants	Who	What	How
Claire	Teacher and one individual student	1. T： What fruit do you like? S1：I like the banana. T：I like bananas.	Recast
	Pair work	2. S：You are girl.（学生多次出现此错误，Claire没有纠错。）	
	Teacher and one individual student	3. S2：You are dog. T： You're a dog.	
		4. S3：I am a small. T：I am small.	

续 表

CF Participants	Who	What	How
Claire	Teacher and one individual student	5. S4：I am a short. T：I am short.	Recast
		6. S4：I am thin. T：I am short and thin.	

Table 9 Observation Checklist of Teachers' Corrective Feedback 9

Participant：Claire

Student：Class Three, Grade Four

Topic：Unit 4, A School Outing — Open Class

Time：June 15, 2014, Sunday

The third observation notes

CF Participants	Who	What	How
Claire	Teacher and one individual student	1. S1：I can see people. T：You can see lots of people.	Recast
		2. T：Can Bob swim? S2：No, Bob can't swim. T：No, he can't.	Recast
		3. S3：The children are very hot. So they are want to buy some ice cream. Bob want ice cream, too. T：The children are very... , no water. Ss：Thirsty. T：Yes, thirsty. The children are very thirsty. （注：Claire按照自己的教学计划来开展活动, 学生说了许多, 出现了许多错误, Claire没有纠错, 而是按照自己的思路去引导学生, 引出预先设定好的thirsty。）	Elicitation

Table 10 Observation Checklist of Teachers' Corrective Feedback 10

Participant: Jane

Student: Class Four, Grade Four

Topic: Unit 8, Helping tourists — Open Class

Time: May 22, 2014, Thursday

The first observation notes

CF Participants	Who	What	How
Jane	Teacher and one individual student	1. T: Where did you go? S: I go to ... T: I went to ... S: I went to the City Stadium.	Recast
	Pair work	2. S1: I want to go to the City ... T: City Stadium. S1: I want to go to the City Stadium.	
		3. S2: Here is the "botel". T: Pardon? S2: "Botel". T: Hotel.	
	Teacher and one individual student	4. T: Which bus goes to the Tianhou Temple? S: Bus 103 go to ... T: Bus 103 goes to ... You say it again. S: Bus 103 goes to the Tianhou Temple.	

Table 11 Observation Checklist of Teachers' Corrective Feedback 11

Participant：Jane

Student：Class Four, Grade Four

Topic：Unit 8, Helping tourists

Time：May 29, 2014, Thursday

The second observation notes

CF / Participants	Who	What	How
Jane	Teacher and the whole class	1. Ss：He is ask the way. T：He is asking the way.	Recast
	Teacher and one individual student	2. S1：Here is the bus stop.（pronunciation） T：Stop. S1：Bus stop.	
		3. S2：We go there by foot. T：On foot. S2：We go there on foot.	
		4. S3：They want to go the bus station. T：They want to go to the bus station.	

Table 12 Observation Checklist of Teachers' Corrective Feedback 12

Participant：Jane

Student：Class Four, Grade Four

Topic：Unit 9, Festivals — Open Class

Time：June 5, 2014, Thursday

The third observation notes

<table>
<tr><th>CF
Participants</th><th>Who</th><th>What</th><th>How</th></tr>
<tr><td rowspan="6">Jane</td><td rowspan="3">Teacher and one individual student</td><td>1. S1：It's our China's holiday.
T：It's our Chinese's holiday.</td><td rowspan="6">Recast</td></tr>
<tr><td>2. S2：I thank for my family.
T：I am thankful for my family.
S2：I thankful for my family.
T：I am thankful for my family.</td></tr>
<tr><td>3. S3：I like April Fool's Day.
Because I can tick others.
T：Trick. Trick others.</td></tr>
<tr><td rowspan="3">Group work
（Jane不打断学生，哪怕有许多错误，只在学生需要时给予帮助。）</td><td>4. S4：I like Halloween. Because I can trick or treat.
T：You can go trick or treating.</td></tr>
<tr><td>5. S5：What is your favourite festival?
T：Which...?
S5：Which is your favourite festival?</td></tr>
<tr><td>6. S6：I like April Fool's Day. Because I can trick on my friends.
T：You can trick your friends.</td></tr>
</table>

Abbreviations

CF	Corrective Feedback
EFL	English as a Foreign Language
ESL	English as a Second Language
SLA	Second Language Acquisition

List of Tables

REFERENCES

[1] AUSUBEL D P. Adult versus Children in Second-Language Learning Psychological Considerations [J]. Modern Language Journal, 1968 (48): 363-420.

[2] BASTURKMEN H. Review of research into the correspondence between language teachers' stated beliefs and practices [J]. System, 2012, 40 (2): 95-282.

[3] BLOOMFIELD L. Outline Guide for the Practical Study of Foreign Language [J].Special Publications of the Linguistic Society of America, 1942.

[4] BOGDAN R C, BIKLEN S K. Qualitative Research for Education: An Introduction to Theories and Methods [M]. Needham and Heights, MA: Allyn and Bacon, 1992.

[5] BOHANNON J N, STANOWICA L. The Issue of Negative Evidence: Adult Responses to Children's Language Errors [J]. Developmental Psychology, 1998 (24): 684-689.

[6] BORG S. Teacher Cognition in Language Teaching: A Review of Research on What Teachers Think, Know, Believe, and Do [J]. Language Teaching, 2003 (36): 81-109.

[7] CARROLL J B. The Contributions of Psychological Theory and Educational Research to the Teaching of Foreign Language [J]. Modern Language Journal, 1996 (49): 273-281.

[8] CARTER K. Handbook of Research on Teacher Education [M]. New York: New York Macmillan, 1990.

[9] CHEN P. Task-Based Teaching of English in Practice: Current Situation and

Prospects [M] .Shanghai: Shanghai Jiao Tong University Press, 2010：61.

[10] CHENOWETH N, DAY R, CHUN A, et al. Attitude and preferences of ESL students to error correction [J]. Studies in Second Language Acquisition, 1983（6）：79-87.

[11] CHUN A, DAY R, CHENOWETH N, et al. Errors, interaction and correction：a study of native-normative conversations [J]. TESOL Quarterly, 1982（16）：537-547.

[12] CHU R. Effects of Teacher's Corrective Feedback on Accuracy in the Oral English of English-Majors College Students [J]. Theory and Practice in Language Studies, 2011（1-5）：454-459.

[13] DEKEYSER R M. The Effect of Error Correction on L2 Grammar Knowledge and Oral Proficiency [J] . Modern Language Journal, 1993（77）：501-514.

[14] DEMETRAS M J, POST K N, SNOW C E. Feedback to First Language Learners：The Role of Repetitions and Clarification Requests [J]. Journal of Child Language, 1986（13）：275-292.

[15] DOUGHTY C. Fine-tuning of Feedback by Competent Speakers to Language Learners [M]. Washington：Georgetown University Press, 1993：96-108.

[16] DOUGHTY C, VARELA E. Communicative Focus on Form [M] // DOUGHTY C. Focus on Form in Classroom Second Language Acquisition. Cambridge：Cambridge University Press, 1988：114-138.

[17] ELLIS R, LOEWEN S, ERLAM R. Implicit and Explicit Corrective Feedback and the Acquisition of L2 Grammar [J]. SSLA, 2006（28）：339-368.

[18] ELLIS R. Corrective Feedback and Teacher Development [J]. L2 Journal, 2009（1）：3-18.

[19] ERICKSON F. Ethnographic microanalysis [J]. Sociolinguistics and Language Teaching, 1996（1）.

[20] MCKAY S L, HORNBERGER N H. Sociolinguistics and Language Teaching [M] . Cambridge：Cambridge University Press, 1998：283-306.

[21] FARRAR M J. Negative Evidence and Grammatical Morpheme Acquisition

［J］. Developmental Psychology, 1992（28）：90-98.

［22］GASS S M. Input, Interaction, and the Second Language Learner［M］. New Jersey：Lawrence Erlbaum Associates, 1997：189.

［23］GASS S, MACKEY A. Stimulated Recall Methodology in Second Language Acquisition ［M］. New Jersey：Lawrence Erlbaum Associates, 2000.

［24］GU P. Understanding teachers as learners：Case study［M］. Beijing：Foreign Language Teaching and Research Press, 2009.

［25］HALLIDAY M A K. Exploring the Function of Language［M］. London：Edward Arnold, 1973.

［26］HU Y Z. Error treatment in EFL classrooms ［D］. Nanjing：Nanjing University, 1999.

［27］HU Y Z. Error treatment in EFL classrooms, Unpublished Doctoral dissertation ［D］. Shanghai：Shanghai International Studies University, 2005.

［28］HYMES D. On Communicative Competence［J］. Sociolinguistics (Selected Readings), 1972：269-293.

［29］HYMES D. Toward ethnographies of communication, In Foundations in Sociolinguistics：An ethnographic approach ［M］. Philadelphia: University of Pennsylvania Press , 1974：3-28.

［30］IWASHITA, N. Negative Feedback and Positive Evidence in Task-based Interaction：Differential Effects on L2 Development［J］. Studies in Second Language Acquisition, 2003（25）：1-36.

［31］JOHNSON K E. The Relationship between Teachers' Beliefs and Practices during Literacy Instruction for Non-Native Speakers of English［J］. Journal of Literacy Research, 1992（24）：83.

［32］JOHNSON K E. The emerging beliefs and instructional practices of preservice ESL teachers［J］. Teaching and Teacher Education, 1994, 10（4）：439-452.

［33］KAGAN D M. Ways of Evaluating Teacher Cognition：Inferences Concerning the Goldilocks principle［J］. Review of Educational Research, 1990.

［34］KAVALIAUSKIENE G, ANUSIENE L. Case Study：Learner Attitudes towards the Correction of Errors [J]. Social Technologies, 2012, 2 (1) : 88-101.

[35] KINZER C K. Instructional frameworks and instructional choices: Comparisons between preservice and in-service teachers [J]. Journal of Reading Behavior, 1988 (10) : 357-377.

[36] LADO R. Language Teaching: A Scientific Approach [M]. New York: New York McGraw-Hill, 1964.

[37] LEU D J, Jr., KINZER C K. Effective reading instruction: K-8 (2nd ed.) [M]. Columbus, OH: Merril, 1991.

[38] LI S F. The Effectiveness of Corrective Feedback in SLA: A Meta-analysis [J]. Language Learning, 2010 (60) : 309-365.

[39] LITTLEWOOD W. Communicative Language Teaching: An Introduction [M]. Cambridge: Cambridge University Press, 1981.

[40] LONG M, INAGAKI S, ORTEGA L. The Role of Implicit Negative Feedback in SLA: Models and Recasts in Japanese and Spanish [J]. The Modern Language Journal, 1998 (82) .

[41] LYSTER R, RANTA L. Corrective Feedback and Learner Uptake: Negotiation of Form in Communicative Classrooms [J]. Studies in Second Language Acquisition, 1997 (19): 37-66.

[42] LYSTER R. Negotiation of form, recasts, explicit correction in relation to error types and learner repair in immersion classrooms [J]. Language Learning, 1998, 48 (2) : 183-218.

[43] LYSTER R. Differential effects of prompts and recasts in form-focused instruction [J]. Studies in Second Language Acquisition, 2004 (26) : 399-432.

[44] MACKEY A, GASS S, MCDONOUGH K. How do learners perceive international feedback [J] . Studies in Second Language Acquisition, 2000 (22) .

[45] MACKEY A, PHILP J. Conversational Interaction and Second Language Development: Recasts, Responses and Red Herrings [J]. Modern Language Journal, 1998 (82) : 338-356.

[46] MACKEY A, OLIVER R, LEEMAN J. Interactional Input and the Incorporation of Feedback：An Exploration of NS-NNS and NNS-NNS Adult and Child Dyads [J]. Language Learning, 2003（53）：35-66.

[47] MARKEE N. Conversation Analysis [M]. Mahwah, NJ：Lawrence Erlbaum Associates, 2000.

[48] MERRIAM S B. Qualitative Research：A Guide to Design and Implementation [M]. Hoboken：Jossey-Bass, 2009.

[49] MILLER L. Japanese and American indirectness [J]. Journal of Asian Pacific Communication, 1994（1-2）：37-55.

[50] OLIVER R. Negative feedback in child NS-NNS conversations [J]. Studies in Second Language Acquisition, 1995（17）：459-81.

[51] PAJARES F M. Teachers' Beliefs and Educational Research：Clearing up a messy constructs [J]. Review of Educational Research, 1992, 62（2）：307-332.

[52] PANOVA I, LYSTER R. Patterns of Corrective Feedback and Uptake in an Adult ESL Classroom [J]. TESOL Quarterly, 2002（36）：573-595.

[53] PHILP J. Constraints on "Noticing the Gap"：Nonnative Speakers' Noticing of Recasts in NS-NNS Interaction [J]. Studies in Second Language Acquisition, 2003（25）：99-126.

[54] RAYANA S, SAOUMA B. The Relationship between Teachers' Knowledge and Beliefs about Science and Inquiry and Their Classroom Practices, Eurasia Journal of Mathematics [J]. Science &Technology Education, 2012, 8（2）：113-128.

[55] RICHARDS J C, LOCKHART C. Reflective Teaching in Second Language Classrooms [M]. Cambridge: Cambridge University Press, 1994.

[56] RICHARDS J C. Beyond Training [M]. Cambridge：Cambridge University Press, 1998.

[57] RICHARDSON V. The Role of Attitudes and Beliefs in Learning to Teach [M]//SIKULA J, et al. Handbook of Research on Teacher Education. New York：New York Macmillan, 1996.

[58] RIVERS W M. The Psychologist and the Foreign-Language Teacher [M]. Chicago: University of Chicago Press, 1964.

[59] SAXTON M. The Contrast Theory of Negative Input [J]. Journal of Child Language, 1997 (24): 139-161.

[60] SCHULTZ R A. Focus on Form in the Foreign Language Classroom: Students' and Teachers' Views Error Correction and the Role of Grammar [J]. Foreign Language Annals, 1966 (29).

[61] SELIGER H W, SHOHAMY E. Second Language Research Methods [M]. Oxford: Oxford University Press, 1989.

[62] SHEEN Y. Corrective Feedback and Learner Uptake in Communicative Classrooms across Instructional Settings [J]. Language Teaching Research, 2004 (8): 263-300.

[63] SMITH D B. Teacher Decision Making in the Adult ESL Classroom [M] // FREEMAN D, RICHARDS J C. Teacher Learning in Language Teaching. Cambridge: Cambridge University Press, 1996: 197-216.

[64] RICHARDS C. Teacher decision-making in the adult ESL classroom [M]. Shanghai: Shanghai Foreign Language Education Press, 2002: 197-216.

[65] STAKE R E. Case studies: In Handbook of Qualitative Research [J]. N.K. Denzin and Y.S., 1998.

[66] STEMPLESKI S, RICE A, FALSETTI J. Getting together: An ESL conversation book [M]. New York: Harcourt Brace Jovanovich, 1986.

[67] THOMPSON C K. Learner-centered tasks in the foreign language classroom [J]. Foreign Language Annals, 1992, 25 (6): 523-531.

[68] TRUSCOTT J. The Case Against Grammar Corrective in L2 Writing Classes [J]. Language Learning, 1996 (46): 327-369.

[69] TSUI A B M. Understanding Expertise in Teaching: Case Studies of Second Language Teachers [M]. Cambridge: Cambridge University Press, 2003.

[70] TURNBULL J, WATERS A. Longman Dictionary of Language Teaching and Applied Linguistics [M]. The Commercial Press and Oxford University

Press, 2010: 490.

[71] WHITE L. Adverb Placement in Second Language Acquisition: Some Effects of Positive and Negative Evidence in the Classroom [J]. Second Language Research, 1991 (7): 133-161.

[72] WIDDOWSON H G. Teaching Language as Communication [M]. Oxford: Oxford University Press, 1978.

[73] WOODS D. Teacher Cognition in Language Teaching: Beliefs, Dedcision-making and Classroom Practice [M]. Cambridge: Cambridge University Press, 1996.

[74] YIM L W. Relating Teachers' Perceptions of the Place of Grammar to their Teaching Practice [M]. Singapore: National University of Singapore, 1993.

[75] Ministry of Education of the People's Republic of China. Compulsory English Curriculum Standards [M]. Beijing: Beijing Normal University Publishing Group, 2011: 2-4.

[76] ZHAO C. Teachers' Corrective Feedback in English Teaching at Different Proficiency Levels: a Corpus-based Study [J]. Journal of PLA University of Foreign Languages, 2005 (3): 35-39.

[77] ZHENG X M, DAVISION. Changing Pedagogy: Analyzing ELT Teachers in China [M]. London/New York: Continuum International Publishing Group, 2008.

[78] ZHENG X M, JIANG Q Y. A Study on the "Teacher's Belief" in the Reform of College English Teaching [J]. Foreign Language World, 2005 (6).

[79] ZHU, M H. Strategies of Error Correction in Oral English Class [J]. Foreign Language World, 1996 (3): 32-33.

ACKNOWLEDGEMENT

This thesis would not have been finished without the help and support of my teachers, families and friends. I would like to take the opportunity to thank the following people.

Firstly, I would like to acknowledge my deepest gratitude to Professor Chen Pei, my supervisor of the study, for her constant and patient guidance, invaluable advice and support. It is Professor Chen who guided me to choose the topic, design the research, collect the data and organize the thesis. It is she who asked me the right questions to get me thinking. I appreciate her responding to and explaining my questions. I would never forget her insightful supervision, assistance and encouragement in my thesis writing.

Secondly, I would also like to thank the other professors and teachers at Shenzhen University, especially Professor Qi, a kind teacher with keen and vigorous academic eyesight and profound knowledge of a wide range of fields, and Mr. Yu Ming, Professor Liu, Professor Guo, Professor Wang, Professor Zheng, and so on. All these teachers inspired me a lot during my study in Shenzhen University.

Thirdly, I want to show my sincere thanks to my warm-hearted classmates and colleagues, who gave me a lot of advice and help.

Last but not least, I am appreciative for my family members' understanding, support and encouragement, my husband and parents-in-law in particular.

The people mentioned above helped me in one way or another and are essential to the completion of my study and thesis. Thanks to them all sincerely and greatly.

